TRADE LIBERALISATION AND ECONOMIC GROWTH IN INDIA

TRADE LIBERALISATION AND ECONOMIC GROWTH IN INDIA

AFAQUE AHMAD KHAN

Neha Publishers & Distributers
Delhi-110002

Neha Publishers & Distributors
4832/24A Prahlad Lane, S-207
Ansari Road, Daryaganj, New Delhi-110002
Tel.: 43570976, 23278261

Ist Edition, 2012

ISBN : 978-93-80318-18-9

Price : ₹ 550/-

Laser Typesetting by : Tamalika Computers, Delhi

Printed at : Nagri Printers, Delhi

PRINTED IN INDIA

Published by Neha Publishers & Distributers, Delhi-110002

Dedication

The Book is dedicated to
my deceased parents
made me enthusiastic
towards higher studies.
May Allah console their souls
in the gardens of Paradise.

PREFACE

Most of the third world countries have a colonial past marked by extensive and intensive exploitation of their economies by the colonial powers. One of the important instruments of this exploitation has been the instrument of foreign trade. Raul Prebisch, Hans Singer, Gunnar Myrdal, Ragnar Nurkse and many other development economists in the forties and the fifties pointed out that the colonial powers have had the best of both worlds, both as consumers of primary commodities and as producers of manufactured articles while the colonies (the underdeveloped countries) have had the worst of both worlds, as consumers of manufactures and producers of raw materials. This was due to declining prices of primary goods and increasing prices of manufactured goods causing the terms of trade to deteriorate considerably over time for the underdeveloped countries (which were exporters primary goods). Therefore many underdeveloped countries that won Independencc in thc post-World War II period viewed foreign trade and investment with a certain amount of suspicion. Therefore they turned their attention to the domestic markets. Many of them also adopted large-scale programmes of industrialisation to build up the industrial sectors of their economies and reduce their dependence for manufactured goods on the developed countries. Therefore the emphasis was on 'inward oriented' policies. As far as foreign trade is concerned, this meant large-scale import substitution (through extensive protection of domestic industries), direct controls on imports and investments, and overvalued exchange rates. As far as export sector is concerned, it was marked by extreme pessimism. For instance, after Independence, the widely prevalent view in Indian government circles was that the Indian exports faced a stagnant world demand and nothing much could be done to increase them.

However, things have now radically changed. Many developing countries adopted programmes of import liberalisation and export promotion in the sixties and achieved remarkable successes. These included Japan, Singapore, Hong Kong, South Korea and Taiwan. The success of these countries has prompted many economists and international agencies (most prominent among them being the IMF and the World Banks to advocate import liberalisation and export promotion as a panaceas for many economises facing developing countries like India. Acting upon their advice, the Government of India opted for a policy of Trade Liberalisation in the 1980 and onwards and has been increasingly dismantling import controls over the last years. The export, import policy measures initiated by the Government of India in global era and economic growth of the country are discussed in this book.

For this volume I am indebted to a number of Teachers, friends, helpers, informants and institutions, without whose help and co-operation, the present work would have remained a dream far me. While it is not possible to express my greatitude to each individually most happily have to acknowledge my indebtedness to a few of them who have been very sincerely associated with my research work.

First of all I wish to express my deep sense of gratitude to my National Leader Shri Sharad Yadava Ji, National President of Janta Dal United (Member of Parliament-Lok Sabha), Convener of N.D.A. without his cooperation, encouragement, it would not have been possible for me to complete this work.

I express my sincere and profound thanks to my dear Socialist friends Javed Raja (National General Secretary of J.D.U. and Dr. Pratyush Nandan Ji (National President Chhatra Janta Dal United) for providing me all facilities in preparation of this volume. I am extremely greatful to Dr. Sunil K. Srivastava for their valuable suggestions for improving this book. I am indeed very greatful and thankful to Nirmal Singh Burchchimal Advocate, 28 old Lawyer Chamber, Supreme Court of India, who always game me not only his affection but kept me inspiring to complete the work.

Finally I am immeasurably indebted to my wife, son Ashab Khan, daughter Fuzaila Khan and my all family members without whose trust, encouragement and forbearance this book would not have been completed.

June 08, 2011 **Dr. Afaque Ahmad Khan**

CONTENTS

CHAPTER-1

INTRODUCTION

Promoting exports has always been a challenge to developing nations, particularly those severely affected by a balance of payment crisis, ever inflating the size of the external debt. India is definitely a case in point. Indian imports have generally outpaced exports, creating significant current account imbalance. Although India didn't do worse than most in terms of external borrowings (Bhagwati and Srinivasan 1993), a natural response of our economic system has been to protect sectors competing with imports through high tariffs and quantitative restrictions. The Indian trade police, till the crisis phase of 1991, was based on three major objectives:

i. To preserve employment in the import-competing sectors;

ii. to raise revenue through trade restrictions; and

iii. to promote self-reliant industrialization.

Hence, the need for reform, that too at a fairly rapid pace. Among the different types of reforms, here we will be concentrating on the trade policy reform.

The trade policy reform really proceeded on three line: first, to drastically reduce the taxes and subsides on exports and imports; second, to relax the quantitative restrictions on imports and exports; and third, adjustment of exchange rates. The import duty was slashed from 150% in July 1991 to 110% in February 1992, 85% in February 1993, and finally to 50% in March 1995. The duty on capital goods, which was 80% in 1991 and varied between 25-35% till 1994, was reduced to 25% in March 1995. The tariffs on project imports for sectors such as coal mining, petroleum refining and power generation were reduced to 25% in February 1993. Similar benefits were provided for import of parts of capital goods (a uniform 15% in March 1995) and all metals, including aluminum (a uniform 25% o in March 1995). Some more retaiolization in terns of auxiliary duty, multiple rates, etc., was carried out in the budget- proposals of 1993 to 1995. The main goal of the above policy has been to provide the so-called "trade neutrality" to exporters so that they can have access to imported inputs free of import duties or other indirect taxes (Levy 1993, p.257). This is reflected in Economic reforms (1993) where high import duties are cited as reasons for

(a) inefficient high cost industries, with uneconomic scales of production, and
(b) high cost of traded inputs leading to high subsidization of exports to make them competitive (p.8).

The second type of trade policy reform, involving moving from quantitative restrictions to tariffs, and then, sequentially, from a high average tariff to a standard, low, uniform tariff, can be taken to be an effort towards boosting import competition (Levy 1993, p.254). In the case of India, import control through licensing has been virtually abolished. However, consumer goods, which largely make up the negative list, can be imported only against licenses. All capital goods, raw materials, intermediates, etc., can be freely imported under open general license (OGL), subjected only to-payment of customs duties, which are being made increasingly unifonn item vise. The thrust of this greater import led competition can be said to be a two-fold attack on:

(a) The heavy protection to domestic industry which breeds inefficiency and discrimination against agriculture and (b) discretionary arbitrariness, abuse and delays which were widespread and put a heavy toll on time, effort and money on small and medium producers (Economic Reforms 1993,p.8).

The third major reform was exchange rate adjustment. It also proceeded-sequentially, whereby into a board-based system of incentive licences (Exim scrips) to exporters (Economic Reforms 1993,p.8). Then the system moved to what is called the Liberalized Exchange Rate Management System (LERMS), whereby 60% of export earnings could be converted to rupees at the open mar-ket rate, allowing a dual rate system to operate. This was taken to be the first step towards full convertibility of rupees in the current account. According to the report of the High Level Conunittee on balance of Payments (RBI Bulletin, August 1993):

The new system attempted to advantages of a relatively stable managed float and the balancing properties of freely floating rate of exchange by creating two exchange rate channels (p.140).

The new system was able to keep the market-determined exchange rate fairly stable and the premium on foreign exchange in the illegal or hawala market fell drastically (to about 8%) (Economic Reforms 1993,p.9).

From 1994, we have witnesses the uniforn rate on current account, whereby the transactions related to education, medical services, etc., have been made free of any restrictions. In the process, however, between end-June 1991 and end-June 1993, the rupee depreciated by 50% vis-a-vis the US dollar (ILO-ARTEP 1993, p.155). This so-called full convertibility on current account was-done in the hope of (1) shifting resources from the non-traded to the traded sector., thereby bringing domestic prices closer to world prices, and (2) providing a powerful incentive to export vis-a-vis domestic production and increasing inward remit-tances from abroad.

The Backdrop

It is quite surprising to note that government documents, even as late as in 1990, were contemplating policies in terms of quantitative restrictions. The Council of Economic Advisors produces a report in December 1989 that pointed out the alarming balance of payments (BOP) position despite high export growth in the previous two or three and a relatively stagnant import growth, all in US dollar terns, during 1988-9. It diagnosed the main cause to be the prevailing macroeconomic imbalance between aggregate demand and supply, leading to inflationary pressures in the economy. Also, this high demand is fuelled further by reckless government budget deficit and increasing RBI credit to the central government by a huge margin. Although the Council speaks in terms of maintaining proper "price relativities of exports and imports", it also favored, equally strongly, quantitative restrictions (Wadhva 1990, p.448).

The major thrust of the Council report (which criticizes government profligacy in expenditure, attributing macroeconomic imbalances to it), is to blame the government export-import policy of the 1980s. According to the Council, this policy, especially the liberal one from 1985-8 allowed an "import-intensive industrialization". As a result (a) there was an increase in the import content of exports, and (b) the direct and indirect foreign exchange requirement grew tre-mendously, especially for consumer durables. Wahva comments: "zit appears that the Council has made the above changes without adequate empirical verification of the issues involved in a comprehensive manner" (Wadhva 1990, p.451). Further, he points out: "there is by now a national consensus on the recommendation of the Council that not only the export growth "must be maintained" but accelerated" Wadhva 1990, p.456). But the crucial question remains that of identifying sectors which are high net foreign exchange earners, because this might not have necessary positive correlation with value added or negative correlation with import-intensive manufacture.

So, the economic reforms pursued in the 1990s have been a culmination of a policy initiated in the mid-1980s. However, the backdrop of this discussion clearly highlights the interdependence of trade reform on other reforms mainly aimed at pruning government expenditure and interference. It also forcefully establishes the fact that blind criticism of liberalized import must be rigorously tested against the net foreign exchange capabilities of our exports. A high growth rate of exports is universally viewed as the need of the day. So the economic reforms in the trade sector, as outlined above, may be taken to be moves in the right direction following a textbook approach. However, several "ifs" and "buts" intervene, some of which are as follows:

i. Most of the measures are basically price measures aimed improving the price competitiveness of exports. But there is a severe dearth of studies,, which analyses the question of competitiveness of India's exports rigorously by segregating the price and non-price factors. Below, we discuss the little stock of knowledge accumulated so far in the regard.

ii. Despite all the doubts expressed regarding the import-intensive content of exports, the value added, and more importantly, net foreign exchange earning of the export items, government and private efforts to carefully study these aspects have been negligible. One of-die major problems seems to be the huge number of input-output coefficients that need to be calculated in order to judge the direct indirect foreign exchange requirements of production for exports or otherwise. Even then, the direct requirements should have been calculated initially; only very recently the RBI and the Export Import Bank of India have undertaken-some studies in this regard. However, not much serious analysis (based on such calculations) has been reported so far.

iii. One of the major problems cited in most of the government and other documents seems to be (a) lack of reforms in the non-tradable sectors which sometimes makes the domestics market relatively more profitable than export. However, these arguments are made without much theoretical insights, so that if the question arises as to what could constitutes the complementary reform of some of the non-tradable infrastructural sectors like power, communications, etc., very little sound responses can be found.

The Scenario in the 1960s

The 1960s witnessed a fairly rapid growth in exports, in contrast to the stagnation in exports throughout the 1950s. Despite this, India could not keep pace wit the growth in world trade, and its share in world exports declined continuously and fell from 1.40% in 1960 to 0.65% in 1970

(Nayyar 1976,p.22). Regarding the commodity composition of export:

i. The declining exports of tea were primarily responsible for the reduced share of food, beverages and tobacco in total exports. Increases in the exports of coffee, oilcakes and cashew kernels did not make up for the loss in the exports.

ii. There was a declined in the percentage share of nearly all the traditional raw-materials exports, such as mica, manganese ore, hides and skin, raw cotton, etc. however, this decline was almost totally compensated for by the extremely rapid increase in iron ore exports.

iii. Although the share of manufactured goods in total exports increase only moderately, the changes in composition within this commodity classification are-very interesting. The traditionally exported manufactured goods were jute products and cotton textiles. All other exports of manufactures can be defined as non-traditional, in the sense that during the 1950s most were relatively insignificant. "the share of traditional manufactures in total export earnings fell from 30% in 1960-1 to 18.8% in 1870-1, whereas, over the same period, that of non-traditional manufactures rose from 11.4% to 31.7%" (Nayyar 1976, pp.24-5).

Following the methodology of Constant Market Share (CSM) analysis, Nayyar commented on different aspects of the export performance of different groups, however, statistically decomposing the different effects (Nayyar 1976):

i. Impact of world demand: The rapid growth of world import demand helped in the growth of exports of cashew kernels, iron ore, chemicals, etc., while the opposite happened in the case of jute manufactures, cotton textiles, tea, tobacco, manganese ore and mica (p.339)

ii. Changes in commodity composition: the contribution of jute manufactures, cotton textiles and tea, which accounted for the bulk of the export earnings during much of the 1960s, lost its importance towards the end of that decade. The share of non-traditional exports of manufactures, like these of engi-neering goods, iron and steel, and chemicals, increased phenomenally during the same period, but 'it did not make up for the stagnation and decline in the foreign exchange earned by the principle traditional exports' (pp .340-1)

iii. Competitiveness: a sharp rise in the cost of raw materials and other inputs, due either to shortages or import substitution policies, posed problems for Indian exports.

Non-traditional exports were boosted mainly by subsides. On the other hand, the pressure of high domestic demand, couples with the higher relative profitability of the home market, seriously affected India's export performance in the 1960s. Supply bottlenecks pose problems for iron ore, raw cashew nuts, manufactured leather, engineering and chemical goods exports in the 1960s (Nayyar 1976, pp.341-3).

About the export policy measures, it is generally agreed that efforts were undertaken to promote non-traditional export, albeit at the cost of traditional export. According to Nayyar the export promotion policies did not properly study the techno- economic feasibilities of new lines of non-traditional export, and narrowed down its range to a very select few. However, these policies, to a certain extent, tried to a very to compensate for the bais of an overvalued exchange rate and the import licensing policies of the 1950s (Nayyar 1976, pp. 344-6)

The question of the impact of devaluation is discussed later, against an overview of the exchange rate management in India.

The Scenario of the 1970s

Nayyar (1976), in the postscript to his book mentions three major reasone for the rapid rise in the rupee value of exports.

i. Steady depreciation in the exchange value of the rupee since 1971

ii. Emergence of Bangladesh as a new trading partner in late 1971.

iii. Boom in the prices of primary commodities, the impact of which was realized in the mid 1970s (p. 352).

If one looks at performance commodity-wise, cashew kernels, tobacco, oilcakes, cotton fabrics, leather (manufactures) and marine products become important export items; incidentally, these were also the industries to suffer domestically. While concluding Nayyar states: 'In sum, the main hypothesis of the book remains unchanged. The problem of India exports is a problem of production. In the ultimate analysis, export can be increased on a sustainable basis only if there is a growth in real national income' (p.376).

India's share of world exports declined almost unabatedly throughout the 1970s. Despite achieving a high volume growth in exports of manufactured goods - 11.2 per cent annum in the 1970s -India still lagged behind the average growth. About the achievement of export growth in the 1970s. Wolf has this comment (1982,pp.50-1):

It can be argued that the essential distinction in the India is that between traditional and non-traditional goods, and not between manufactured and non-manufactured goods. Although there are many new categories of export such as engineering goods, garments, iron ore, iron and steel, handicrafts (especially polished diamonds), finished leather, oilcakes, marine products, and sugar, few achieved a sustained high rate of growth over a long period, and where a comparison was made, India's growth did not match that of its major competitors, especially in newer manufactured exports.

To investigate the reasons for the above pater, four overlapping, but competing, hypothesis are discussed:

i. Initial commodity composition did not match with the growing sectors in the world demand.
ii. The production of exportable grew slowly in relation to the domestic absorption of those products.
iii. Growth of world demand itself was slow.
iv. Slow growth of exportable surplus was not the cause of slow growth of exports but, rather, highlighted the distorted incentive studies (Wolf 1982, pp.55-6).

Wolf strongly believes that the last one is the major hypothesis, which should be analyzed seriously. This is because the first two hypotheses can be said to be not the cause of slow exports, but rather the choice of the policy- makers aiming at self -sufficiency. Wolf tried to prove throughout his book that the policies adopted by the Indian government were thoroughly biased aginst exports. The bias against imports as well also led to a production structure, which used domestic inputs (at distorted prices).

Before going into industries of policy parameters in the 1 1970s, Wolf categorized industries into those basically export oriented and those exporting negligibly. Among the highly export oriented industries, he included iron ore, ore, tea, coffee, cashewkemels, pepper, fine cured

Virginia tobacco jute products, leather and leather manufactures and polished diamonds. Also important were clothing, frozen shrimp and oilcakes.

In marginal export contribution he identified chemical machinery, transport equipment, metal products and basic metals (mainly iron and steel), tobacco (other than fine cured Virginia), sugar and cotton textiles (pp,46-7).

In the mid -1970s the following important incentive schemes were valid (Wolf 1982, ch.4):

i. The cash Assistance Scheme aimed at offsetting either domestic taxes or the Duty Drawback Scheme, or the difference between short run marginal cost and realized export price.
ii. Import Replenishment Licences (REPs) made available scarce foreign under limited conditions.
iii. The Duty Drawback Scheme, that was devised to repay the exporter for excise and import duties levied on his inputs. It was given exclusively to manufacture exports other than machinery and transport equipment and chemicals.

The above incentive schemes, however, precluded long run planning because cash assistance was announced quarterly, REP premiums were highly variable, and duty drawbacks were inadequate in periods of inflation. On the other hand , import quotas, relatively profitable to produce for domestic profitability. Thus it was always relatively profitable to produce for domestic markets-rather than to export. Imports were largely restricted to non-competitive producers' goods and certain mass consumption goods, especially food.

So what should be the policy goal of the Government? After analyzing different cases in India, especially the efforts to increase exports first and then to liberalize. But for long-term success, the bias against exporting has to go. Wolf suggests the following sequence.

Replacing quantitative restrictions by tariffs; then replacing the tariffs and export subsidies by an export rate adjustment combined with a reduction in the variance of incentives. Success with such a policy would depend crucially on maintaining highly competitive exchange rate throughout (Wolf 1982, p. 148).

The trend of exports in the early 1990s – and subsequently – has closely resembled such a package.

Another important work on this period, by Bhagwati and Srinivasan (1976), concluded that the devaluation of 1996 was good because relative profitability in exports increased. It supported the thesis that excess capacity in industries helps in the growth of exports. In fact, increased export duties offset the 'gross' devaluation by a large margin, making the 'net' devaluation smaller.

The increased availability of imports following import liberalization also helped in boosting the production of exportable and shifted the export supply curve outwards. In one of the most interesting approaches, Bhagwati and Srinivasan calculated the static allocation and efficiency impact on growth. The measure used was DRC (domestic resource cost), which is [ERP (effective rate of protection) + 1], where r=number of Indian rupees per dollar. DRC is 'broadly indicative of difference in the returns to deployment of domestic resources, using the approximation that observed unit export values measure true opportunity cost to society' (Bhagwati and Srinivasan 1976, p.177). Non-food consumer goods had the highest DRC followed by capital goods. The high variance of DRCs among industries, according to the authors, 'does indicate that the system is sub-optimally organized ... the system is indeed designed to ignore opportunity c ost in making allocational decisions' (p. 183).

The Scenario of the 1980s

The 1980s began with a disastrous balance of payments (BOP) scenario for India. Some import liberalizatio measures for capital goods and intermediates in the late 1970s led to higher imports of these commodities. The high inward remittance from abroad, however, helped to ease the BOP situation. But the rise in oil prices in 1979 gravely aggravated the BOP problem. Joshi and Little (1994) have produced the most comprehensive work on the BOP situation in India by evaluating a number of points of view. India entered into the controversial SDR 5 billion loans from the IMF, which required fulfillment of conditionalitiesregarding fiscal and monetary variables. However, according to Joshi and Little (1994), evidence points to the unsatisfactory performance of exports and the concurrent appreciation of real exchange rate. The slow-down in world trade, due to world recession during 1980-2, is being held as one of the major causes for this. Joshi and Little (1994) rebutted the logic, as the developing- let alone the dynamic exporting - countries performed much better than India from 1979-80 to 1985-6. While aggregate exports increased in volume by about 2 per cent per year, non-oil exports were virtually stationary between 1979-80 and 1984-5, and there was actually a fall in the comparable figures for convertible currency areas. The volume of exports of manufactured goods fell between 1978-9 and 1982-3, as that of engineering goods fell between 1978-9 and 1984-5. the value of export earnings in dollar terms also stagnated due to slow rise in export prices. (Ibid., p. 157).

The lack of strong policy regarding real exchange rate

(RER) led to an appreciation in RER. So it was, too, with the problems regarding a fall in the inflow on account of invisibles (which fell due to a decline of net earnings from transportation and tourism), interest payments to the IMF, and the end of the Gulf boom in 1980-1 (Ibid., p. 160). The situation was made worse by the poor performance of public and corporate savings, leading to the increasing demand for foreign capital inflow by the strong demand for private investment, further fuelled by the strong demand for private investment and by reckless government spending. According to Joshi and Little, import liberalization, instead of depressing the current account balance, actually helped in its improvement by increasing exports through the provision for essential imported components.

Export performance from 1985-6 to 1989-90 was very good. The dollar value of exports increased by about 14 per cent a year, the volume of exports by 12 per cent and that of manufactured exports by 15 5 per cent. According to Joshi and Little, this mainly achieved by depreciating the currency to a lower real effective exchange rate. The increase in export subsides from 9 to 13 per cent during the same period depreciated the Indian rupee by almost 40 per cent (Ibid., p. 183). Among non-quantifiable measures, the liberal import of capital goods allowed to the exchange porters, is understood to be most important by Joshi and Little. They also tried to improve that the exchange is the most important determinant of Indian competitiveness. They used a simultaneous equation framework to separately estimate export demand and supply equations. The export demand was functionally related to the volume of India's exports, to world income, and to the relative prices of Indian and world exports., to domestic prices of the same, and a domestic excess demand tem. Their result shows export supply elasticity to be 0.7

in the short-run and 1.1 in the long run, with 80 per cent in the first two years respectively. From these they conclude:

These results show that India is not and expression to the general presumption that the price-competitiveness of exports is an important determinant of the volume of exports and the relevant elasticities are more than adequate for a real depreciation to improve the current account even with a zero price elasticity of demand for exports (1994, p.275).

We shall discuss these issues in the chapter on competitiveness, and its relation to depreciation of real effective exchange rate in a subsequent chapter. It will suffice to note that the analyses by Joshi and Little are not fully defensible as (a) they are vague regarding the concept of competitiveness, which should be clearly stated before the above strong judgments are made, and (b) they are ready to discuss the lower bound of export elasticities (which exists in the presence of a number of controls in the willing to do the same for imports- without this, the lower bound effect on the trade balance, of such price measures like depreciation of real effective exchange rate, cannot be calculated.

From the preceding analysis, we can infer that the export promotion policy in India assumed an important role over the years in order to improve the current account account trade balance. However, and exclusive stress on price competitiveness led to manipulation of export prices through subsidies and incentives. Scant attention was paid to non-price factors in export competitiveness, which is crucial. The serious dearth related to the measurement of India's competitiveness and the role of price and non-price factors amply testifies to this. Somewhat related to this is the attitude towards import liberalization, which was supposed to ease the need for imported inputs of exporters. At the same time, as a long- term goal, net foreign exchange capabilities of industries were taken to be very important for achieving stability in the current account trade balance. The achievement of this goal requires a careful study of the import-intensive content of experts and its relation to the net foreign exchange earning potential of particular industries. A comparison of export industries on the basis of their growth, net foreign exchange earnings potential and import content seems essential, but such an exercise is sadly missing in most of the studies.

The major problem, mentioned somewhat. earlier, is the rather piecemeal treatment of the non-tradable sector in the export promotion policies. It is argued that monopoly and rigid pricing in the non-tradable sectors prevents the realization of full effect of price competitiveness. This is reflected by the rather satisfactory movement of the measure of real exchange rate, which takes into account relative's prices of tradable and non-tradable. Hence, the question remains: what should be the proper policy towards non-tradable? A simple switching expenditure from non-tradable to tradable will not help. But if more competition in the non-tradable sector were introduced by allowing private sector participation through a judicious policy-mix regarding output and pricing, it would be more complementary to trade sector reforms. A strong infrastructure, with suitable allowances for the essential supply it needs to provide, might generate the requires flexibility in the competitive movement the real exchange rate.

Macroeconomic Perspectives

The potential influence of excport promotion on ecionomic growth, for a country such as India. Policies which target significant growth in exports, are often driven by the motivation to improve overall economic conditions. The views that export policy can be a catalyst of national economic growth received a ma-jor boost from the recent experiences of the East Asian nations. Even industrial-ized nations, such as USA, Japan and those of Western Europe, have been ac-tively pursuing different types of export – subsidizations schemes over a considerable length of time Time and again such policies are justified because they are likely to increase e employment; national income investment and long-term economic growth. An interesting example is the 'National Export Strategy' report presented to the US congress in 1994 by the Trade Promotion Coordinating Committee, which repeatedly asserts that the export support programs are meant for a 'better US economy. The recent thrust of India's trade policy aims at a commendable, sustained long-run growth of exports. Hence, it becomes extremely important to identify the avenues through which growth in exports can increase the rate of growth for the economy as a whole. Before we get into a discussion of the Indian scenario, let us take a brief detour in seeing the availability analyses of exports in relation to economic growth.

In a significant paper, Michealy (1977) used simple rank correlation on a 41-country sample for 1950-73 to analyze whether the rate of growth of exports has been associated with GD, growth. In order to avoid spurious correlations, because export itself is a part of GDP, the rank correlation used 'export-share' as the crucial variable. Spearman's coefficient was significantly positive for the group as a whole. It was larger for a sub-sample of middle-income countries. Balassa (1987) found positive correlation between different measures of the rate of growth of exports and output growth. 'However, these studies did not address the casualty issue and there was no sound theoretical basis for these studies.

Feder (1983) used a neoclassical growth model to study the impact of export growth on the rate of growth GDP by hypothesizing a positive externality effect of export growth. This was captured by the inclusion of exports as an additional productive factor in the production function of the non-export sector. Then he used a sample of 31 semi-industrialized countries and found evidence of positive impact of exports on growth. Helleiner (1986) has strongly argued that a minimum level of development is required before the benefits of export promotion can be realized. A number of studies showed that the coefficient of export growth was significantly larger for the middle-income group. For poorer nations, the contributions of export growth in explaining growthin income have not been that significant. Kohli and Singh (1989) have investigated whether a 'minimum critical threshold' related to the trade structure itself, rather than income pre capita can distinguish countries. Using data on 41 countries, they have shown that the coefficient of export growth was significantly lager for the outward-oriented nations. Edwards (1993) nicely summarizes the findings of the existing literature:

In sum, most studies have found that in GDP growth regression the impor-tance and significance of the exports growth varies across groups of countries, causing some doubt on the desirability of pooling all these nations together in the econometric analysis. However, it is unlikely that this issue will be further evaluated until more sophisticated econometric techniques are used on pooled time-series-cross section data.

Theoretical papers dealing with the possible impact of export promotion on macroeconomic variables in a developing economy are scare, at least relative to the numerous empirical papers in this area. Much research is needed to isolate and identify exact routes through which exports can provide stimulus to national income and employment. Feder (1989) focuses on supply-side issues. For example, it is the supply-side link between exports and non-exports that leads to growth (Feder, 1989). On the other hand, earlier Keynesian models emphasized the role of export demand in generating higher output and employment in an excess-capacity economy. The question is, what theoretical framework befits the Indian experience - a question that is almost impossible to answer. A pure Keynesians framework does not allow for much price adjustment. Hence, the supply-side constraints operating on the export sector are entirely absent. Larger external demand always generates additional output and employment Structuralist macroeconomics often relates the rate of utilization to the degree of capac-ity utilization to give a 'long-run' flavor to the standard Keynes-Kalecki models. Hence, greater export demand, by increasing the degree of capacity utilization, would boost the growth rate. Whatever be the supply-side implication of export growth, one can't deny the beneficial effects of export growth on the traditional export products. Labor-intensive exportable may require a boost in demand to utilize unemployed human resources. Yet, the main focus of growth should be on the rate of investment, that is, whether an export bonanza can uplift investment share so that the one-time impact is magnified through a second- round investment boom. A point that should be noted here is that the successful Asian exporting ration also exhibited significant savings investment proportion in the GDP. In fact, a simple Keynesian model could be quite insightful for this purpose. Consider an economy with excess capacity where savings and imports are given in the following specifications:

$S = sY,$ $0<s<1$ 1

$M = mY,$ $0<m<1$ 2

Exports are determined exogenously by the demand, worldwide"

x=X 3

Where investment demand function takes the following form,

$I = \hat{I}$ for $Y= Y$ 4

= á (Y). Y for Y>Y

á?>O, á?<0

Condition (4) retains the basic feature of a simple Keynesian frame-work and modifies it by an accelerator relationship. Once *Y* goes beyond threshold level *Y*, investment demand starts responding to output. Investment demand as is exhibit here is partially driven by 'animal spirit' and partially responds to actual output levels. We have assumed that the investment func-tions is concave in *Y* for *Y* > *Y*. There is no compelling reason for the assump-tion of concavity. In fact, if a was constant, we could guarantee stability by assuming *á* < *s*+*m*. Since we are dealing with a Keynesian framework, all the action is taken place away from and below the full capacity output level. If *Y* the full employment level of output, we are contemplating that as *Y* approaches *Y*, incentive to invest diminishes. For stability it is assumed that

á (Y) at *(Y= Y)* < *s*+*m* 5

We are now in a position to detennine the equilibrium level of income *Y* which is given by

$$Y_e = I+X \qquad 6$$

Considering *Ye* < *Y* and an increasing in *X*. It alters *Ye* by *(?X)/(s+m)* provided the new *Ye* is also lower than *Y*. On the other hand, if *Ye* > *Y*, an increase in *X* would be responded to by a greater increase in Ye since the multiplier is changed to 1/[s+m-á(.)]. This is fairly obvious because a boom in exports induces a second-round increase in the level of investment. This exposition talks about a one-time' movement rather than the entire growth path. The point is that i a rise in exports in a Keynesian system induces further expansion it investments, lemand output response would be much stronger. Therefore, outcome is nainly dependent on the nature of investment function. If investment responds rigorously to capacity utilization only after the utilization reaches critical point, export expansion may have to traverse a long way before it stimulates investment. ['o understand the relationship between export growth and growth in- output it rust start with the following basic relation ship:

$$Y = X+D \qquad 7$$

There Y is GNP, X is the total exports and D is domestic demand or domestic component of aggregate demand, using to denote proportional change, it gets

$$Y = \ddot{e}X + (1-\ddot{e})\,D. \qquad 8$$

Where 0<*ë*<1, (8) does not suggest any theory for determining the rela-tionship between X and Y however, if it assumes that the aggregate X is entirely determined exogenously, which is usually done in a typical Keynesian frame-work, a growth in X would determine the other variables. Moreover, there has to be a positive relation between X and Y, provided the share of exports in GNP is positive,. The ideas are that an increase in X has a multiplier effect on Y just a positive correlation between

X and Y does not suggest that it would be signifi-cant. In fact, for export share to be very low an increase in X would have a negligible impact on Y But whatever it is in a Keynesian framework, it is impos-sible that X and Y would be negatively correlated.

In a supply-constrained economy, where Y is more or less determined from the supply side, X and D would be inversely related. An increase in D will force X to come down and vice-versa. Just for argument's sake one can think of a situation where producers are quite reluctant to export and would concentrate only on the internal market. After the domestic market is saturated, they would sell the surplus in the global market. Hence, export would be determined as a residual. Growth of D would be negatively correlated with a growth in X, an if the share of exports in GNP is low, growth in Xand Y would be moving in oppo-site directions. As one can see, this is the exact opposite of the Keynesian model. Exports don't act as a driving force, but as a residual. Most of the empirical works in this area try to decide whether a significant relationship exists between growth in exports and growth in output, without really looking into the macroeconomic conditions that dictate such a relationship. It is just described two possible situations with a typical Keynesian and a non-Keynesian flavor. This has been done to reflect on the experience of the Indian economy prior to the initiation of the current reform process.

Whether a country should follow an inward-oriented Policy has been one of the highly debated issues in Development Economics. Raul Prebisch and Gunnar Myrdal are prominent among those who strongly advocated as in word-oriented policy for the developing countries. While Raul Prebisch's Thinking influenced the trade policy of Latin American Countries, Myradal's thinking is said to have influenced India's trade policy in the early years of planning era. The experience of many developed Countries, which benefited from protection and sequrol spe-cial problems which the developing countries faced prompted many economists to transform the infast industry argument of advanced countries into young economy argument in the context of developing economies. France followed a vigorous policy of protection and the industrial expansion faciliated by this was used as a spring board for the capture of export maket. Japanese experience also proved that for this country a break away from the Asian patterns of Stagnation and powerty would not have been possibled if an inward-oriented policy had not been vigorously followed. Latin American Countries followed import-Substitution Strategy in the 1950's and similarly south Korea and Taiwan also initially followed. this policy The socialist countries were known for their autarkic policy. All this obviously has tremendous influence on India's trade regime in the early years of planning era.

Independent India, infact, inherited on inward-oriented policy and in the early years of planning an import-substitution regime with antiexports bias considered to be quite appropriate for India. The aim of import-substituting policy was to become independent of imparts in respect of machinery and to restrict imports to only raw materials and intermediate manufactures. This policy was also coupled with high levels of duties on imports to protect the domestic indus-tries. As pointed out Bhagwati and Srinivasan, "The planners clearly assumed that a policy of autarky was not only possible but also desirable. It was in keeping with this doctrine that for many years imports were subject to restrictive bureau-cratic control and that the significace of exports for the growth of the economy as a whole was understimated. "Imports were permitted only in case of those goods which were indigenously not availabe. This system provided a high degree of protection to domestic industries.

India's trade regime remained basically inward-looking unit export incentives were introduced in the mid sixties. But the policy of impots prohibition on imports and the controls imposed on investment and the import-substituting policy practically continued till the oil crisis of 1973. In the seventies many more export incentives were introduced and also exports obligations was imposed on the industries at the various stages of licensing. This however, did not help exportpromotion much. The eighties again witnessed attempts again witnessed attempts towards export promotion and trade liberalisation under sixth and seven Quantitative restrictions were replace by tariffs; producers got easy access to imported inputs and many items were place on open general licence (OGL) list and all this marked a move towards further liberalisation of the trade regime. The long-term Fiscal policy of 1985 suggested that quantitative restrictions should be continued for some more time only in the case of industries which are just establishing themeselves and that all capital goods, intermediate goods, raw materials and components should be imported subject to tafiff and that the import duty structure must be simplified. But all these attempts towards liberalisation did not dismantle the system of controls and therefore this could at best be described as slow and hesitant move towards trade liberalisation.

Despite the efforts towards liberalisation in the seventies and eighties, the degree of openness achieved was for from adequate and India's trade regime more or less remained inward-looking.

According to Srinivasan, "If examined with reference to the rates and du-ration of protection closely, there whould be no parallel to Indian situation. Rarely, if ever, tariffs of 100 percent or more and sustained over as long a period as three decades as in India were granted in the history of the U.K. Germany, U.S. or even France, the traditional bastion of protectionism. Besides high tariffs India has imposed quantitative restrictions on imports, a policy that has few parallels in the economic history of those countries."

What is the impact of the inward looking policy pursued by India? Self reliance was perverted into self-sufficiency and irrespective of comparative advantage, attempts were made to replace imparts by domestic production. Across-the board import substitution followed for too long a time has done more harm than good to the Indian economy.

First stage of import-substitution which involves production of non-durable consumer goods is quite justifiable since it does not result in efficient production because of the fact that only unskilled labour could be sufficient and also the problem of economies of scale does not arise. But as one moves to the second stage of import substitution which involves domestic production of durable goods and intermediate goods to replaces imports reduiring the use of highely skilled labour, modern technology, large scale production etc. the disadvantage of import substitution becomes evident. In the postwar period several countries including India pursued the second-stage import substitution and under this policy, they embarked on the production of commodities that less and less conformed to their comparative advantage.

Under the umbrella of protection, the disadvantage of infancy was not overcome, instead inefficient and high cost production structure was encouraged and India could not become competitive in the world economy. This had its adverse effect on exports as well. Export prices received were lower resulting in the ad-verse effect on the production of export goods. Because of rapid change in tech-nology, import-substitution was not much of a sucess in Capital good sector. Industries actually become more import dependent and consequently import substitution did not actually reduce import requirements. With poor performance of the exports sector, the country could not earn the required amount of foreign exchange needed in the process of development and external borrowing become necessary which made the country highly indebted. This disadvantage of an inward-oriented strategy become more and more obvious in the eighties with the marked shift in manufacture in favour of consumer durable which required more imported inputs, but lacked international competitiveness.

The unprecedented balance of payment Crisis witnessed in the first quarter of 1991-92 complled the policy-makers to think of a major departure from the trade policy follow till then and to make a serious move towards further integration of the Indian economy with the rest of of the World. The disenchantment with the inward-looing policy experienced by several countries and the sucess of the outward-looing policy particularly in the newly industrialised in favour of India adopting a similar policy. Latin American countries which pursed inward-looking policy were disenchanted with it and started liberalising their economies through they did not succeed much in this. Soon after the second world war Den-mark and Norway followed outward-oriented policy. Southern

Europe and Japan in the mid fifties and Korea, Singapore and Taiwan in the early sixties went in for outward-oriented policies and achieved tremendous success. These countries gave freedom to their entrepreneurs to choose between domestic and imported inputs and duty-free imports of inputs were permitted. As open economies they become highly competitive and very substantially increased their exports and achieved higher rate of growth. Studies conducted by Michaley, Balassa and Michalopoulous and jai have shown that countries more open to world trade have higher GNP growth rates or in other words they have shown that there is positive association between the degree of openness and GNP growth. It has also been found that exports of manufactures create more employment for the same amount of values added than does the production of import-competing manufactures. Anne Krueger and other have provided empirical evidence in support of this on the whole, experiences of those countries which adopted on outward-looking strategy have established the fact that capital productivity and growth rates are higher in open economies than closed economies.

It has been shown that in India, even with hesitant liberalisation efforts of the eighties, productivity performance of the industrial sector could be improved. Ahluwalia has shown that after a long-term decline of 0.3 percent per annum in the sixties and seventies, total factor productivity in the organised manufacturing sector increased at the rate of 2.5 percent per annum in the eighties. Further, improvement in the export of engineering goods and chemicals in the second half of the eighties has been attributed to the liberalised import regime for exports.

At a time when India was facing economic crisis, the

experience of Newly Industrialising countries and her own experience of newly industrialising coun-tries and her own experience with limited liberalisation in the eighties clearly pointed towards the urgent need for further integration of the Indian economy with-rest of the world as a solution to poor performance of the economy and accordingly some new measures have been intiated since July 1991.

Theoritically the relationship between foreign trade and economic growth can bi a positive, a negative, and elective one. The positive views has been help by the classical and neo-classical economists. According to them foreiggn trade is an engine of economic growth" On the other hand, structuralists believe that international trade has actually operated to the deteriment of the poor countries cousing deterioration in their terms of trade. In between the two extreme positions lies the electic view which incorporates some elements of each of the op-posing view points. According to this view exports can act as a stimulus to the rest of the economy under certain favourable conditions. Foreign-trade may also serve as a logging sector of the economy. In this case the stimulus to development is internal and trade may slow down growth. Nurkese believes that growth in the underdeveloped. Countries should proceed through domestic industris should proceed through domestic industrialisation, because there is little Chance of reliance on exports-led growth. Nurkse further adds that the productivity in agriculture sector must also increase, otherwise increased from manufactures will be partly spent on food stuff and thus create pressure on imports or cause inflation.

W. Arther Lewis (1980), holds the view that the engine of growth is trade only, we have to change of source of fuel for the working of the engine. In the past, it was fueled by industrial grow in developed countries but since the mid 1970s the developed countries are expenriencing a secular decline in the rate of economic growth. This emphasizes the need to turn to an alternative sources of fuel which according to Lewis, lies in trade among the developing countries. The view expressed World Bank have should that trade can serve as an effective source for promoting economic growth only if it si carried in Multilateral framework i.e. trade between "South" and "North" and not only between "South -South" or "North-North".

Many emprical studies have been undertaken to findout the relationship between exports and economic growth. Among all these studies, prominent are Emergy's (1967) Michaely (1977); Heller (1978), Balassa (1978), Aderlmen (1984) and chow (1987). These studies establish .very strong and positive link between exports and economic growth. Most of the developing countries followed the exports-oriented stategy of development in order to reap the economies of scale for their industries and to increase the extent of the market or to have access to foreign markets to sell their products. The acknowledged sucess of outward oriented development in South Korea, Taiwan, Singapore and Hong-Kong etc. is party responsible for the move towards market based policies. Moreover, the developed countries recognise the role of trade in prompting growth and industrial development in the low and middle-income countries. As a result of this many developing countries have significantly liberalized trade in the course of their bread structural adjustment programes. These reforms have benefited the countries taking them.

India during the last four decades followed the policy of industrialization through import substitution. The adoption of import substitution strategy of development was influenced by the consideratins of "size" factor and also because of "export panimism"

The Mahalotiobis Model of development adopted in the second-five year plan visualized no role for international trade in economic growth. It was based on the assumption of a relatively closed economy. In subsequent plan periods, India become highly "controlled" and an "isolated" economy having the very high rates of effective protection, in the range of 100 to 200 percent or even more. This led to very inefficient domestic industries and very high prices for domestic consumers. The heavy protection and subsidies to industry lead to ex-cessive capital intensity and relatively little labour absorption and thus generally aggravating the unemployment and under-employment problems. In India im-port substitution has been coined to far.

Methodology

For the emprical varification of the effect of export and import on economic growth of a country is done with the help of multiple requressions analysis using the secondary source of date published in economic sureys and R.B.I. Bulletin from various issues. We shall test the hypothesis that whether income changes with respect to changes in export or impor or not this will be tested by Calculations of income elasticity of export and income elasticity of import of defferent components of exports and import of India.

The proposed research work runs through the following chapters. At first will be introduction: Introduction will analysis the importance of openess of the economy for the rapid development of of it. Further It will-locate the research gap that esists in the Indian economy. In the sphere of international trade under this heading analysis of methodology will be done. Which will carry on impirical verification. Chapter planning-will -be also there to make the study sistmatic.

Chapter one will deal with India's foreign trade since 1962 in a historical prospect chapter. Second will give us foreign trade and economic growth in a therotical setting undoutadly therotical setting undoutadly theory makes the base for the analysis of impact of the foreign trade on economic growth.

Chapter third makes clear the position of foreign trade in India during the study period.

For the Improvement of the trade and veaping the benefit of foreign trade what policy had been followed by Indian govt. will be analysed in -the chapter fourth under the heading of foreign trade policy of India.

In the chapter five impirical verification will done dealing with the func-tional analysis of income and export and income and import. Further In will carry on the test. The responsiveness of income and export and income and export and that of import under the different categorical heading of India. Finally chapter six will deal with the conclusion and suggestions found out in the process of study of the proposed research work.

CHAPTER-2

INDIA'S FOREIGN TRADE SINCE 1962 TO 1992: AN HISTORICAL ANALYSIS

For study of trends of India's foreign trade during post-independence period, it is convenient to divide the entire period into seven phases.

1948-49 to 1950-51-On the eve of Planning

On the eve of planning, the foreign trade of India showed an excess of imports over exports. The rise in imports was largely due to (a) pent-up demand of the war and post war period as a consequence of various controls an restrictions, (b) the shortage of food and basic raw materials like jute and cotton as a result o partition, (c) the rise in the imports of machinery and equipment -or capital goods-to meet the growing demand for hydro-electric and other projects started during the period.

1957-52 to 1955-56- The first Plan Period

The annual growth average value of imports during the First Plan Period was Rs. 730 corers and that of exports Rs. 622 corers. In this way, the average annual trade deficit worked out to be Rs. 108 corers. Trade deficit was largely due to programs of industrialization, which gathered momentum and pushed up the imports capital goods. There was no-improvement in exports.

Table: Trade Balance during First Plan

(Rs. Corers)

Year (April -March)	*Imports c.i.f*	*Exports f.o.b*	*Balance of Trade*
1950-51	650	647	-3
1951-52	963	730	-233
1952-53	633	602	-31
1953-54	592	540	-52
1954-55	690	597	-93
1955-56	773	641	-133
Total 1951-52 to 1955-56	3651	3109	-542
Annual average	**730**	**622**	**108**

Source: Reserve Bank of India Bulletins.

1956-57 to 1960-61 The second Plan Period

During the second Plan Period, a massive program of industrialization was initiated. This included the setting up of the steels plants, heavy expansion and renovation of railway and modernization of many industries, and as a result; the quantum of imports reached a very high level. Besides this, the maintenance imports required for a developing economy further increased our imports. Food grains imports had to be resorted to overcome internal shortages and rising prices.

Export earnings averaged Rs. 613 corers per annum. (Refer table 3). The figure of average exports earnings for the Second Plan was lower that that under the First Plan, which-shows that, the much-needed diversification of exports and exports and export promotion drive did not materialized. Consequently, the trade balance become heavily adverse to the tune of Rs. 467 corers which was in sharp contrast to the moderate trade deficit of the order of Rs 108 corers per year during the First Plan. Foreign exchange crisis become acute during the Second Plan Period.

1961-62 to 1965-66 The Third Plan Period

The record of exports during the Third Plan shows that the average exports earnings worked out to the Rs. 747 corers. (Refer table 4). As against it, actual annual average imports worked pout to be Rs. 10224 corers. The increase in the volume of imports during the Third Plan was due to three factors. Firstly, rapid industrialization necessitated larger imports of machinery, equipment, industrial raw materials and technical know-how. Secondly, the defense needs had increased following aggression by China and Pakistan. Finally, larger quantity of food grains was imported, partly because it was easily available and partly because of extensive failure of crops in 1965-66.

Table : Trade Balance during Second Plan

(Rs. Corers)

Year (April-March)	*Imports c.i.f.*	*Exports f.o.b.*	*Balance of trade*
1956-57	1102	635	-467
1957-58	1233	594	-639
1958-59	1029	576	-453
1959-60	932	627	-305
1960-61	1106	631	-457
Total 1956-57 to 1960-61	5408	3063	-2339
Annual Average	**1080**	**613**	**-467**

Source: Reserve Bank of India Bulletin.

Devaluation of 1966 and the period up to 1973-74

Persistent adverse balance of trade since 1951 and consequent adverse of balance payments, acute shortage of foreign exchange, extensive borrowing by India from foreign countries and international institutions like IMF to overcome balance of payments problems-all these factors included India to de4vluate the rupee by 36.5 per cent in June. 1966. Devaluation was resorted to essentially (a) to reduce the volume of imports, (b) to boost exports, and (c) create a favourable balance of trade and balance of payments. Since devaluation was announced during a year of drought and the following year again happened to be a bad weather year as was also the year when the government announced its policy of liberalizing imports in case of 59 industries, the immediate effect of devaluation was the further aggravation of the trade deficit. Although after devaluation of the rupee, exports increased during 1966-67 and 1967-68, but on account— of relative inelasticity of imports, the import bill literally soared-Rs. 10992 corers in 1966-67 and Rs. 2.043 corers in 1967-68. as a consequence, the balance of trade situation worsened during 1966-67 and 1967-68. However, with a better crop during -1968-69. Food grain imports declined. Moreover, devaluation also produces its healthy effect in stimulating exports. Consequently, balance of trade, which was unfavorable to the tune of Rs. 788 corers during 1967-68, declined significantly during the next three years. As a consequence of policies of imports restriction and reduction in food grain imports could with vigorous measure of exports promotion, during 1972-73, the country was able to have a favorable balance of trade for the first times since Independence. This was a healthy development but its impact was soon lost in 1973-74 because of several international factors, which pushed up the prices of petroleum products, steel and non-ferrous metals, fertilizers and newsprint. Although the spurt in the prices of exports helped to boost them up to a level of Rs. 2.523 corers, the kick given to imports was much stronger they reached a high a level of Rs. 2.955 corers. Consequently, deficit in the trade balance of the order of Rs. 432 corers appeared again in 1973-74. in an overall sense, trade magnitude as compared with the period of the second Plan. Third Plan and the Annual Plans.

Table : Trade Balance during 1961-62 to 165-66

(Rs. Corers)

Year (April-March)	***Imports c.i.f.***	***Exports f.o.b.***	***Balance of trade***
1961-62	1006	668	-338
1962-63	1097	681	-416
1963-64	1245	802	-443
1964-65	1421	801	-620
1965-66	1350	783	-567
Total 196-1-62 to 1965-66	6119	3735	-2384
Annual Average	**1224**	**747**	**-477**

Source: Reserve Bank of India Bulletin. March 1947

Table : Trade Balance during Annual Plans, the Fourth Plan

(Rs. Corers)

Year (April-March)	***Imports c.i.f.***	***Exports f.o.b.***	***Balance of Trade***
Annual Plans			
1966-67	1992	1086	-906
1967-68	2043	1255	-788
1968-69	1740	1367	-373

Contd...

Total 1966-67 to 1968-69	5775	3708	-2067
Annual Average	**1925**	**1236**	**-689**
Fourth Plan			
1969-70	1582	1413	-169
1970-71	1634	1535	-99
1971-72	1824	1607	-217
1972-73	1867	1971	+104
1973-74	2955	2523	-432
Total 1969-70 to 1973-74	9862	9049	-813
Annual Average	**1972**	**1810**	**-162**

Note: Figure are based on Director General of Commercial Intelligence and Statistics.

Source: Reserve Bank of India Bulletin. December 1981 and other issues.

1974-79: The Fifth Plan Period

The hike in oil prices, which started in October 1973 seriously, affected the pattern of trade throughout the world and India was no exception. Table 5 shows how the value of imports during the fifth Plan period reached very high levels- largely the result of a sharp increase in the cost of India's major imports viz., petroleum, fertilizers and food grains. Simultaneously, there was a significant improvement in India' exports as they successively rose every year during the Fifth Plan period. The rise was so fast that by 1976-77, exports at Rs. 5.146 corers exceeded imports by Rs. 72 corers - balance of trade surplus emerged for the second time since 1951. Exports of fish and fish preparation, coffee, tea, groundnuts; cotton fabrics and readymade garments and handicrafts recorded substantial increase in this period.

Another interesting point of this period was that during 1977-78 and in the next two years,, the Janata Government followed a policy of haphazard import liberalization at a time when exports boom had almost petered out- the result was the re-emergence of the trade deficit from 1977-78 onwards.

Table: Trade during the Fifth Plan

(Rs. Corers)

Year	*Imports c.i.f.*	*Exports f.o.b.*	*Balance of trade*
1974-75	4,519	3,329	-1,190
1975-76	5,265	4,043	-1,222
1976-77	5,074	5,146	+72
1977-78	6,025	5,404	-621
1978-79	6,814	5,726	-1,088
Total 1974-75 to 1978-79	27,697	23,648	-4,049
Annual Average	**5,540**	**4,730**	**-810**

Source: Reserve Bank of India Bulletin, December 1981.

1980 onwards: The Sixth and Seventh Plan Period

With the last year of the Fifth Plan (1978-79), trade deficit started widening. On account of a further increase in the prices of petroleum products by OPEC the import bills shot up from Rs.6,814 corers to over Rs.8,908 corers in 1979-80 and further to Rs.12,524 corers in 1980-81 and to Rs.13,608 corers in 1981-82. Though exports too continued to rise, the value of exports fell much short of imports. The result was unprecedented trade deficits-from nearly Rs.2,450 corers in 1979-80 to Rs.5,813 corers in 1980-81. It was this yawning deficit, which forced the Government to approach the IMF in November 1981 for huge loan.

Table: Trade Balance during Sixth and Seventh Plans

(Rs. Corers)

Year	*Imports c.i.f.*	*Exports f.o.b.*	*Trade Balance*
1979-80	8,908	6,459	-2,449
Sixth Plan			
1980-81	12,524	6,711	-5,813
1981-82	13,608	7,806	-5,802
1982-83	14,356	8,908	-5,448
1983-84	15,763	9,872	-5,891
1984-85	18,680	11,959	-6,721
Total 1980-81 to 1984-85	74,931	45,256	-29,675
Annual Average	**14,986**	**9,051**	**-5,935**
Seventh Plan			
1985-86	21,164	11,578	-9,586
1986-87	22,669	13,315	-9,354
1987-88	2502	16,396	-9,296
1988-89	34,202	20,647	-13,555
1989-90	40,642	28,229	-12,413
Total 1985-86 to 1989-90	1,44,369	90,165	-5411204
Annual Average	**28,874**	**18,033**	**-10,841**

Source: Economic Survey (1991-92) and Reserve Bank of India Bulletin, March 1993.

The same situation continued in 1983-84 and the trade deficit further rose to about Rs.5,891 corers. A review of the data of imports and exports reveals that despite the fact imports of POL declined from Rs.5,267 corers in 1980-81 to Rs.4,830 corers in 1983-84, partly because international prices of oil showed a downward trend and partly because domestic production of crude was jacked up by ONGC, the trade deficit was of the order of Rs.5,891 corers in 1983-84. This is explained by fact that declined in POL imports was more than counterbalanced by a big hike in non-PL imports as a consequence of the policy of import liberalization. The figures of 1984-85 indicate a further deterioration in the balance of trade and the trade deficit was of the order of Rs A 721 corers. The annual average imports during the Sixth Plan (19880-81 to 1984-85) were of the order Rs.14,986 corers. Consequently, a huge annual average trade deficit of the order of about Rs.5,935 corers was witnessed during the Sixth Plan.

Data about the Seventh Plan period (1985-86 to 1989-90) reveal that on account of the policies of indiscriminate liberalization being followed by the Congress (I) government and later endorsed by the Janata Dal Government, the average annual imports a shot up to Rs.2,874 corers, but exports averaged Rs.18,033 corers. Thus an unprecedented annual average trade deficit of the order of Rs.10,841 corers emerged. The huge trade deficit compelled the Government to approach the world Bank/ IMF for an unprecedented loan of over $ 6.7 billion. The Government was also forced to apply brakes on the licensing policy of import licenses.

India's Foreign Trade- 1989-90 and thereafter

During 1990-91, according to DGCI&S figures, there is no doubt that a push was give to our export effort and exports shot up to Rs.32,558 corers in 1990-91 indicating an increase of 17.7%, but as a consequence of the Gulf War, the Government failed to curb imports and they reached a record level of Rs.43,193 corers- an increase of 22.6 per cent. As a result of the sharp increase in imports, trade deficit shot up to a high figure of Rs.10,635 corers.

Table: India's Balance during 19879-90 to 1993-94

In Rs. Corers | In US $ million

	Exports	*Imports*	*Trade Balance*	*Export*	*Imports*	*Trade Balance*
1989-90	27,658	35,328	-7,670	16,612	21,219	-4,607
1990-91	32,558	43,193	10,635	18,145	24,073	-5,928
1991-92	44,042	47,851	-3)809	17,866	19,411	-1,545
1992-93	53,688	63,375	-9,687	18,537	21,882	-3,345
1993-94	69,751	73,101	-3,350	22,238	23,306	-1,068
1994-95	82,674	89,971	-7,297	26,330	28,654	-2,324
1995-96	106,353	1,22,678	-16,325	31,797	36,678	-4,881
1996-97	118,817	1,38,920	-20,103	33,470	39,132	-5,662
Annual Average (1992-93 to 196-97)						
	86,257	97,609	-11,352	26,474	29,930	-3,456
1997-98	130,101	1,54,176	-24,076	35,006	41,484	-6,478
1998-99	141,604	1,76,099	-34,495	33,659	41,858	-8,199
1998-99	139,753	178,332	-37,579	33,219	42,389	-9,170
1999-00*	162,738	200,062	-37,324	37,556	46,169	-8,613
Annual Average Growth Rate (1992-93 to 1999-00)						
	17.7	19.6	9.7	11.4		

Provisional

Source: Compiled and computed from the data provided in Reserve Bank of India Bulletin, March 1996 and August 1999.

During 1991-92, exports in dollar terms showed a decline by 1.5% compared with 1990-91, from $ 18,145 million in 1990-91 to $ 17,866 million in 1991-92. But import compression was much sharper by 19.4 % from $ 24,073 million in 1990-91 to $ 19,411 million in 1991-92. Despite the fact that the Government introduced a number of measures in the new trade policy allowing exims scrip, abolishing cash compensatory support (CCS) schemes as also a two- step devaluation of the rupee, but these measures failed to boost up exports. Even the growth in exports to the General Currency Area (GCA) rose by 6.34% during 1991-92. However, exports to Rupee Payment Area

(RPA) during 1991-92 declined by 42.5% in dollar terms. This was largely due to the difficult politi-cal situation in the erstwhile Soviet Union leading to its disintegration. Consequently, exports did not pick up but resulted in a decline.

During 1992-93, exports rose by merely 3.7% in dollar terms- from 7,866 million in 1991-92 to $ 18,537 million in 192-93, but as a against them, imports increased by a much larger margin of 12.7%- from $ 19,411 million in1991-92 to $ 21,882 million in 1992-93. Consequently, balance of trade deficit, which was of the order of $ 1,545 million in 1991-92 rose to high figure of $ 3,345 million in 1992-93. Several factors were responsible for the worsening trade deficit. Firstly, the import of oil rose by 13.6% and peaked to $5,624 million in 1992-93. Secondly, with the removal of import compression measures, imports recover and this also added the import bill. On the export front, the exports to the General Currency Area (GCA) rose by 10.4% in 1992-93. This was largely due to a response to a liberalized trade and exchange rate regimes. But exports to the Rupee Payment Area (RPA) declined by 62.2% in the previous year. Thus was due to th continuance of economic uncertainties in the former Soviet Union. This had an adverse effect on boosting exports.

An analysis of the 8-year period 1992-93 to 1999-00) reveals that although export effort picked up to 1995-96 - a" first rate and exports jumped from US $ 17,866 million in 1991-92 to 31,797 million 1995-96 an increase of about 78 % during a short span of four years. But simultaneously, policies of liberalization accompanied with reduction of custom duties resulted in increase of imports from $19,411 million in 1991-92 to $ 36,678 million in 1995-96 - an increase of about 89%. Consequently, the trade deficit which was of the order of $1,545 million in 1991-92 increased to $ 4,881 million in 1995-96-it rose by over three times.

Thereafter, as a result of the sharp deterioration in world economic environment in trade, the South East Asian crisis, continued recession in Japan, severe economic crisis in Russia in 1998 and fall in world output by 2% during 1997-98 leading to a decline in the world trade. During 1998-99, exports decline to $ 33,219 million as against $35,006 million in 1997-98. However, exports picked up during 1999-00 to $ 37,556 million. Coreresponding1y, there has been a much a sharper increase in imports from $ 36,678 million during 1998-99 to $ 46,169 million during 1999-00. The benefits of exports growth had been more than neutralized by sharper increase in imports and as a consequence, trade deficit reached the unprecedented level of $9,170 million in 1998-99 and $ 8,613 million in 199-00. During the 8-year period (1992-93 to 1999-00), the annual average increase in exports was of the order 9.7% and that of imports was 11.4% (in dollar terms).

It may, however, be noted that provisional estimates are based on DGCI & S data and do not take into account the defense imprts. Consequently, when RBI figures based on actual shipment of bills would be available, the trade deficit would be still larger. To that extent, the trade deficit figures underestimate the trade gap.

Another point which deserves serious attention In that in rupee terms, exports rose by 17.6 per annum (compound) during the 8-year period (1992-93 to 199-00) and imports rose by 19.6% per annum. (Refer Table 8) but much of the export effort was frittered away in neutralizes the effect of the two-step devaluation undertaken in 1991 and the rise of the value of imports was also to a large extent the result of the devaluation of the Rupee. Obviously, devaluation is only a short-term measure- a palliative; it does not offer an enduring solution to our problem of continuing trade deficit. For this purpose, it would be more desirable to exercise a strong control on the rise of prices in India so that the Rupee in the international market does not become overvalued again and thus necessitate another devaluation. The cure lies in making our economy grow at a faster rate so that inflation can be controlled effectively. This can help the export effort becoming really effective.

Trends in Value of Trade since Independence: *Salient Points*

We may summarize the whole analysis by emphasizing the salient features:

Growing value of trade. In the first place, the total value of India's international has gone up from Rs.1.250 corers in 1989-50-51 to nearly Rs. 19,000 corers in 1980-81 and to Rs. 3,18,085 corers in 1998-99. But much of this increase was concentrated in the last 10 years or so. For instance, between 1951 and 1971, the total value of foreign trade rose only 2.5 times; it was only between 1974-75 and 1998-99 that there was considerable increases in the total value of India's trade. This is explained by increase in the quantum of trade as well as rise in the prices of goods constituting imports and exports. The continuously rising value of trade brings out-the significance of international trade for the Indian economy and with a higher degree of economic development and diversification of the economy, the value of trade is bound to increase still further, in spite of this tremendous growth India's share in world trade was 0.61% in 1997 which was less than that of small countries like Taiwan and Singapore. In 1950-51, how-ever, India's share was 2.1% of world trade.

Larger Growth of India's imports. Secondly, the value of India's imports has been continuously rising since 1951, for various reason reasons, such as:

i) rapid industrialization necessitating increasing imports of machinery and equipment, industrial raw materials, technical know-how, etc;
ii) regular import of fooedgrains from 1958-59 to 1972-73 under P.L. 480 to supplement domestic production and thereafter, to maintain certain level of buffer stocks of food grains;
iii) control of inflationary pressure within the country through increased imports and supply of price sensitive goods such as edible oils, cement, etc;
iv) policy of libèral imports on the pretext of exports promotion, resulting an increse of not only essential imports but even non-esential imports such colours T. V , etc;and
v) periodic hike in crude oil prices of OPEC since 1973 from a little over \$2 to nearly \$27 per barrel, constituting the single biggest factors for boosting imports since 1973-74 and especially till 1979-80.
vi) Policy of import liberalization pursued during 1985-86 and thereafter.
vii) The disquieting factor here is that the unit value of imports has risen much factor than the quantum index.

Inadequate expansion of exports. during the first three plans, there was no increase in exports- in fact, there was even a decline. It was only during and after the Annual Plans, exports really started picking-up. One reason why India's exports were always stagnant during the first 15 years of planning was the predominance of traditional goods such as tea, jute and cotton manufactures, the foreign demand for which was generally inelastic. Besides, the rise in prices in India and the high cost of production of our export goods did not allow these goods to be competitive in the international markets.

After devaluation of the rupee in 1966, Indian export goods got a price advatage. Moreover, the Government entered into a series of bilateral agreements with socialist countries which gave a boost to our exports. The Government introduced a series of Ifiscal and cash incentives to boost exoports. Finally, iot set up a number of export promotion councils and agencies to promote exports. These factors explain the rapid growth of ex\ports in the 1970s. but the increease in exports was never adequate and accordingly, exports matched imports only in two years in the last five decades. There were many reasons why our effort effort did not match our import requirements:

i) The major export items of India were till recently agriculture-based and the prices of primary goods generally remained low in the international commodity markets, mainly because the demands of developed countries for these goods was inelastic and partly due to failure of primary goods producing countries acting together;

ii) the ever-increasing domestic consumption and inadequate export surplus in certain commodities, e.g., sugar, vegetables, meat, etc. the demand for which has been rising;

iii) export promotion measures, such as tax and other incentives were found inadequate, particularly in the context of larger incentives provided even by advanced countries like Germany and Japan;

iv) the policy of protection adopted by advanced countries such as USA preventing the full flow of exports from developing countries;

v) long period of business recession in recent years in most developed countries, resulting in sluggish international demand; and

vi) the unit value of exports has risen much more than the quantum index of exports, showing that the increase in the value of exports was partly monetary. But then, the rise in the unit value of imports was much greater than the unit value of exports.

vii) In 1980-81, exports as percentage of GDP were only 5.5%, in 1990-91, this ratio increased to 6.2% and by 1995-96, it further improved to 9.2%in 1999-00. This implies the growing importance of exports for the Indian economy. However, imports which were 10.2% of GDP in 1980-81, declined to 9.4% in 1990-91, but rose further to 11.3% in 199-00. There is a need to prone inessential imports so that the benefits of sharp increase in exportscanbe translated into positive balance of trade.

Widening trade deficit. Except for two years, when India had mar-gin trade surplus, she has experienced deficits throughout this period, and what is worse, the annual average trade deficit which was only Rs. 108 corers during the First Plan rose to Rs. 467 corers during the Second Plan, to Rs. 747 corers during the Third Plan and to Rs.689 corers during the Annual Plan period. It was only during the Fourth Plan period that-a real and successful attempt was made to reduce the trade deficit by restricting imports on the one side and boosting exports on the other and results was that annual average deficit came down to Rs. 162 corers during the Fourth Plan. The Fifth Plan period reversed the trend of the Fourth Plan and witnessed the upward increase of both import and ex-ports- trade deficit rose to Rs. 810 corers. Since then, the opposition has almost gone out of control- for example, trade deficit during the Sixth Palm period has averaged

Rs.5,935 cores average per annum. The situation has worsened further and annual average trade deficit during 1985-86 to 1989-90 was of the order of Rs.10,8412 corers. During 1992-93 and 1997-98, average trade deficit was of the order of Rs.11,352 corers. This indicates further deterioration during the Eight Plan.

There has been a slowing down in the growth of both imports and exports during 1997-98 an 1998-99. More probable factors during the period 1992-93 to 1998-99 for the slowdown in exports are: (i) depressed natures of world market (ii) saturation of developed countries markets for electronics goods which have been among the most dynamic exports sectors, and (iii) increased protectionism by industrials countries on area of textile and clothing (despite GATT and WTO). However, on the import front, recless import liberalization has contributed to mounting and burgeoning import bills.

Table: Annual Increase in Exports and Imports during 1995-96 to 1997-98

(US $ million)

	Exports	*Growth (%)*	*Imports*	*Growth (%)*
1995-96	31,795	20.8	36,675	28.0
1996-97	33,470	6.3	39,132	6.7
1997-98	35,006	4.6	41,484	6.0
1998-99	33,219	-5.1	42,389	2.2
1999-00	37,556	13.0	46,169	8.9

Source: Compiled and computed from the data given in RBI Bulletin, June 2000.

Despite several concession and incentives provided by the Com-merce Ministry, exports have not picked up, though Commerce Ministry is still struggling to give a kick-start to the economy and especially the export sector to reach the export growth target of 20% during 1999-00. The data reveal that dur-ing 1999-00, exports rose by 13% in dollars terms, but they're a statistical fal-lacy in this figure, since exports had declined to $33,219 million in 1998-99. There are several factors contributing to this situation. Firstly, India underestimated the impact of South-East Asian crisis during 1997-98, but this sis now considered to be major contributing factor among the causes of export growth slump. Although India's trade with this region accounts only 8% of India's total export growth, but its indirect effects have to be taken into account. Secondly, there is an increasing competition from China and Taiwan. Thirdly, exports of textiles have also-been affected by the restrictive and protectionist policies of developed countries on the one hand and increasing competition from China on the other. Fourthly, large industrial houses have miserably failed to boost exports. A study of 500 top companies made by Commerce Ministry has revealed that large industrial houses account for only 5% of total exports, while their import intensity is very high. In other words, large industrial houses are net losers of foreign exchange. Fifthly, the service sectors in the Indian export market have made some headway, for instance, software exports rose by 65% during 1997-98 reaching a record level of Rs.6,800 corers, but their contribution to total exports isstill small (5.4% of total). Sixthly, the developed countries to slowdown Indian exports have created non-tariff barierrs. The use of anti-dumping duties by these countries has also affected exports. Recently gray cloth exports- a major product from India has come under anti-dumping duty in the European Union for five years. This had a very adverse effect. All these factors have contributed to the sharp slump in the export market.

Table : Structure of Indian Imports

Annual Compound Rates (per cent)

	1970-71	1980-81	1990-91	197-98
I. Bulk Imports	82 (50.5)	8,739 (69.6)	19,464 (45.1)	54,965 (31.2)
A. Petroleum, Crude & Products	137 (8.4)	5,267 (42.Q)	10,816 (25.0)	27,064 (15.3)
B. Bulk Consumption goods	326 (20.0)	901 (7.2)	966 (2.2)	9,600 (5.5)
a. Cereals and Pulses	213	100	1,301	1,383
b. Edible Oils	39	704	326	7,131
C. Other Bulk Items	362 (22.1)	2,571 (20.5)	7,650 (17.7)	18,301 (10.4)
a. Fertilizers	100	818	1,766	4516
b. Non-Ferrous	119	477	1,102	2,823
c. Paper -Paper	456	1,891	9.3	19.5
d. Metallic Ores	11	116	1,528	2,550
e. Iron & Steel	147	852	2,113	4,956
II. Non-Bulk Imports	809	3,472	23,729	1 ,21,130
C. Capital Goods	404 (24.7)	1,910 (15.2)	10,471 (24.2)	38,570 (21.9)
a. Machinery except	258	1,089	3,768	13,073
b. Electrical & electronic goods	70	260	1,702	11,227
c. Transport equipment	66	472	1,670	2,571
d. Project goods	-	-	2,556	8,609
D. Mainly Export Related items	193 (11.8)	1,158 (9.2)	6,603 (15.3)	29,791 (16.9)
a. Pearls, Precious Semi Precious stones	25	417	3,738	15,827
b. Organic & Inorganic Chemicals	131	673	2,289	11,435
c. Textiles, yarn and manufacturers	8	59	443	1,836

Contd...

d.Cashew nuts	29	9	134	693
e. Others	212 (13.0)	404 (3.2)	6,655 (15.4)	52,769 (30.0)
Total (I+II)	**1,634** **(100.0)**	**12,549** **(100.0)**	**43,193** **(100.0)**	**176,099** **(100.0)**

Source: Compiled and computed from RBI, Report on Currency and Finance (1998-99)

Composition of India's Foreign Trade

In view of the fact that the Directorate general of Commercial Intelligence and statistics (DGCI&S) has revised the commodity classification of India's foreign trade wit reference to 19987-88, trade data before and after 1987-88 are not strictly comparable. We have made an effort to adjust the data for the year 1970-71 and 1980-81 as per revised classification so that it provides some basis of comparison.

Pattern of Imports

Imports have been now classified into bulk Imports and non-bulk Imports. Bulk imports are further subdivided into three components-(i) Petroleum, crude and products, (ii) Bulk consumption goods which comprise of cereals and pulses, edible oils and sugar, (iii) other bulk items comprising of fertilizers, non-ferrous metals, paper and paper board, rubber, pulp and waste paper, metallic ores, iron and steel.

Non-bulk imports are also further classified into three components - (1) Capital goods which include metals, machine tools, electrical -and non-electrical machinery, transport equipment and project goods, (ii) Mainly export-related items consist of pearls, precious and semi precious stones, organic and inorganic chemicals, textile yarns and fabrics, cashew nuts, (iii) Other includes artificial resins and plastic material, professional and scientific instru-ments, coal and coke, chemical-medicinal and pharmaceutical products, non-metallic mineral manufactures etc.

A close perusal of table 9 reveals that there has been a per-sistently raising the trend of imports, which is the result of both internal and external factors. During the seventies, as a result of sharp hike in oil prices by the organization Petroleum Exporting Countries (OPEC) first during 1973-74 and then again 1979-80, the value of POL imports rose sharply not only during the seventies, but its impact was felt even during the eighties as well. The economy also suffered a major drought in 1979-80.

During the eighties, a number of factors produced a culminate in pushing up imports. Notable among them were: a higher outflow of foreign exchange consequent among the hike in POL prices as a part of legacy of the preceding decade, severe shortages on account of the unprecedented drought of 1987, the growing pressure of demand accompanied with the stepping up of the real growth of the economy and the policy of liberalization adopted by the Gov-ernment. All these factors set in motion a process, which led to relatively larger dependence of the economy on imports. Imports which aggregate to Rs.1, 634 corers in 1970-71 rose sharply to Rs.12,549 corers in 1980-81, the annual growth rate was as high as 19.2% during the decade. During the eightes abd more espe-cially after 1984-85 when Prime Minister Rajiv Gandhi followed the policy of liberalization, imports zoomed formed to Rs. 43,190 crores in 1999-91. During 1990-91 and 1998-99, imports, grew at the annual rate of 19.6 per cent.

It is customary to blame the POL items for the rise in imports, while this was largely true during the seventies, the experience of the eighties revaals that the average annual growth of POL items was barely 7.4% during 1980-81 to 1990-91, but the overall growth of imports was of the order of 13.1 per cent per annual. The explanation of a repaid increase in impotts has, therefore, to be sought in terms of the policy of liberalization in the congress (1) government. During 1990-91 and 1998-99, growth rate of POL items by 22.6% per annum. This was largely due to the over-zealous policy to boost up automobile production, which increased POL imports.

Bulk imports, which comprised basic raw materials, intermediates and foodstuffs, are linked to the growth and stabile of the economy, at an annual average growth rate of 23.2 per cent during the seventies. As a result, their share in total imports went up from 50.5 per cent in 1970-71 to 69.6 percent in 1980-81. However, their rate of growth significantly declined during the eighties as well as during the nineties.

Among the non-POL bulk items, consumption goods comprising cereals and cereal preparation, edible oils, pulses and sugar declined at an an-nual growth rate of 8% during the Seventh Plan period. However, imports of iron and steel product recorded a much higher growth rate of 14.4% per annum during 1985-86 to I990-91, but declined thereafter during 1990-99.

By and, a large, the growth of bulk items decelerated during the Seventh Plan to 7.2% as against 10.2% during the Sixth Plan. Consequently, the share of bulk items in total imports fell to 58.6% in 1985 a further declined to 31.2% in 1998-99. Among which had slumped down to 15.2% in 1980-81 started picking up and was of the order of about 17.7% during 1990-91 and 1998-99.

Consumer goods and food grains. The imports of consumer goods and food grains accounted for 40% of India's import during the First Plan period, showing the

Table: Average Annual Imports pf Principle Commodities

(Rs. Corers)

Items	*1951-52 to 1960-61*	*1961-62 to 1965-66*	*1966-67 to 1968-69*	*1969-70 to 1973-74*	*1974-75 to 1979-80*	*1980-81 to 1984-85*	*1985-86 to 1989-90*	*1990-91 to 1997-98*
1. Food grains	141	241	400	196	548	374	516	415
2. Machinery (Including locomotive)	191	472	518	484	1078	2515	6415	13,598
3. Minerals oil	77	85	90	226	2063	5264	4498	23,717
4. Metals (Ferrous and non-ferrous)	93	172	185	309	647	1448	2450	6,540
5. Chemicals drugs and medicines	44	55	126	113	254	660	1868	7,945
6. Fertilizers	-	28	121	96	439	698	1114	6,055
7. Pearls and Precious stones	-	-	-	-	244	730	2405	8,137

Source: Reserve Bank of India Bulletins and RBI. Report on Currency and Finance, 1997-98.

extent of India's under-development and her dependence on foreign countries even fore a basic necessity like food grains. But the imports of these have gradually declined over the years- 35% during the Second and Third Plan period, 27% during the Fourth Plan and 25% during the Fifth Plan and only 12% during the Sixth Plan (1980-81 to 1984-85) and 2.5% during the Seventh Plan, but declined significantly to 0.7% during 1990-91 to I998-99.

From 19578 onwards, imports of food grains were considerable these were arranged through PL480 Aid from USA. Till the beginning of the Fourth Plan, India's imports of foodgrains as a percentage of total imports were increasing. Food grains imports increased because of the drought conditions inability domestic supplies to meet fully domestic demands. It was only during the Fourth Plan that imports for food grains declined to I01%. In fact, with the accumulation of larges reserves of food grains, their imports were virtually elimi-nated in certain years during 1970's and they are minimal in 1980's. Thus, the structural changes in imports since I951 show:

(a) rapid growth of 'industrialization necessitating increasing im-ports of capital goods raw materials,
(b) growing imports of raw materials on the basis of liberalization of imports for exports promotion; and
(c) declining impotr4ts of food grains and consumer goods due to country becoming self-sufficient in food grains and other consumer goods through agriculture and industrial growth.

Trend of Principal Imports

Food grains- The imports of food grains were necessitate by the partition of the country and the growing demand for food for the rising population. The average annual imports of food grains, which were about Rs.120 corers during First Plan, rose to Rs, 161 corers during the Second plan, further increased to an average rate of Rs. 24I corers during the Third Plan. The drought of 1965-66 further worsened the situation and consequently, food grains imports worth Rs. 1,201 corers were made during the there years, i.e. 1966-67 to 1968-69. During the Fourth Plan, a declining trend in food imports was observed. Food import bill, which was of the order of Rs.184 corers in 1969-70, went down as low a figure as Rs.28 corers only. But these were four good crops years. The trend was reversed in I973-74 when food imports jumped to Rs. 746 corers. On an average, food imports of the order of Rs.548 corers were made during the period 197-75 to 1979-80. With a bumper crop of food grain and with a large buffer stock created food grain s imports have dwindled since then. During the five-year period (1980-81 to 1984-85) food grains imports averaged about Rs.374 corers per annum. In 1987-88, food grains worth Rs. 66 corers were imported- a negligible figure indeed. But during 1992-93, food grains worth Rs.1,240 corers. Even during I998-99, food grains worth Rs. 1,383 corers were imported.

Machinery- Imports of machinery include electrical non-electrical equipment as also locomotives. In a country, which is rapidly industrializing her economy, imports of machinery are bound to increase. Compared to the average annual import of machinery was about Rs.191 corers during the 1951-61 to 1960-61, the average annual during the Third Plan rose to Rs.472 corers. During 1974-75 and 1979-80, value of machinery imports averaged Rs.1,078 corers. Machinery imports averaged Rs.2,515 corers per annum during 1980-81 to 1984-85. Their annual average jumped Rs.6,415 corers during the Seventh Plan (1985-86 to 1989-90). They further went up to Rs. 24,300 corers during 1998-99. The increasing import of machinery is and indicator of our growing industrialization as well as our failure to develop our own technology and indiscriminate liberalization in import policy.

Minerals Oils- imports of mineral oils are also on the increase. India is short in the supply of mineral oils, especially petroleum. Annual import of mineral oil during 1969-70 to 1973-74 averaged Rs.226 corers. On account of the sharp increase in the prices of crude announced by the Organization of Petro-leum Exporting Countries, during 1973-74 one, petroleum imports were of the order of Rs.569 corers. Their annual average during 1974-75 to 1979-80 was of the order of Rs.2,063 corers. During 1980-81 to 1984-85 imports of petroleum, oil and lubricants rose to very high level- the average annual value of POL im-port bill was Rs.5,264 corers. During 1998-99, import of mineral oils reached a recorded level of Rs.27,064 corers.

Metals- India imports iron and steel and also non-ferrous metals. The average annual imports of ferrous and non-ferrous metals, which were about Rs. 54 corers during the First Plan, have gone up steadily with every plan and are about Rs.2,450 corers during g 1985-86 and 1989-90. Imports of metal on such a large scale are necessitating by vast program s of industrial expansion, development of railways and hydroelectric_ projects. With improvement in capacity utilization of our steel plants, imports of iron and steel should be cut down. During 1998-99, metal worth Rs.8,972 corers were imported as against the annual average of Rs.6,540 corers during the 1990-91 to 1997-98.

Chemicals, drugs, and medicines- there have been an increase in the imports of chemicals, drugs and medicines. The average annual of these items was about Rs.55 corers during the Third Plan. Imports of Chemicals, drugs and medicines rose to Rs.113 corers per annum on the average during the Fourth Plan. During 1980-81 and 1984-85 annual average imports of this item rose to Rs.660

corers. It further rose to Rs.1,868 corers during 1985-86 to 1989-90. They rose further to Rs.14,543 corers during 198-99.

Pearls and precious stones- the import of pearls and precious stones averaged Rs. 223 corers during 1974-79 and they have further increased to Rs.2,405 corers per annum for the period 1985-86 to 1989-90. Part of these imports is meant to satisfy the demand of the affluent sections and part of these imports serve as raw material for the handicrafts export-industry. It may be noted that the exports of pearls and precious stones were of the order of Rs.24,839 corers during 1998-99, as against an imports of Rs.15,834 cores.

Fertilizers- following the adoption of the New Strategy in Indian agriculture, the imports of fertilizers were stepped up. The average annual im-ports of fertilizers, which stood at Rs.28 corers during the Third Plan, rose to Rs.121 cores during 1966-67 to 1968-69 but with the increase of domestic pro-duction of fertilizers, imports on account of this item declined to an annual average of Rs.96 corers during the Fourth Plan. With a sharp increase in the interna-tional prices of fertilizers, annual average imports of fertilizers during the Fifth plan were of the order of Rs.423 corers. During 1980-810 to 1984-85, the annual imports of fertilizers were of the order of Rs.698 corers. As a consequence of liberalization, fertilizers imports jumped to Rs.1,436 corers in 1985-86 and were of the Rs.1,114 cores per annum -on an average during 1985-86 to 1989-90. Imports of fertilizers were of the order of Rs.4,516 cores in 198-99.

Pattern of Export

Exports of India are broadly classified into four categories: (i) Agriculture and allied products which include coffee, tea, oilcakes, tobacco, cashew kernels, spices, sugar, raw cotton, rice, fish, and fish preparation, meat and preparation, vegetables, fruits, vegetables and pulses; (ii) Ores and minerals include manganese ore, mica and iron ore; (iii) Manufactured goods includes textiles and ready-made garments, jute manufactures, leather and footwear, handicrafts including pearls and precious stones, chemicals, engineering goods and iron steel's and (iv) mineral fuels and lubricants.

Data given in table 12 reveal that traditional exports dependent upon agriculture and mineral wealth accounted for 42% of total exports in 1970-71 their share has, however, declined to about 21% in 1998-99. As against it, the share of manufacture has gone up from about 50% in 1970-71 to about 77% in 1998-99. Obviously, the structure of Indian exports is changing in favors of manufactured goods whose share has gone up from about 51% in 1970-71 to about 77% in 1998-99.

Exports of Principal Commodities

Tea and coffee- Tea and coffee are important items of Indian exports. Tea had the first position in our exports in certain years. The average annual exports of tea were Rs.106 corers during the First Plan period. Tea exports further picked up to touch Rs.195 corers in 199-60-61. But later they declined. Tea exports earned Rs.1,132 corers during 1991-92, but their contribution rose to Rs.2,302 corers in 1998-99.

During 1998-99, coffee exports touched a record level of Rs.1,703 corers.

Cotton Yarn and Manufactures- during the First plan period, the average annual export of cotton yarn and manufacture touched Rs. 81 corers, but they decline to small figure Rs. 55 corers during the Third Plan. On account of relatively high cost in Indian textile industry, India found it difficult to capture the international market. In each high cost were due to rising labor cost and use of old and worn-out machinery. In the post-devaluation period exports of cotton textiles have increased on account of their competitiveness in the international market. During 1970-71 and 1998-99 exports of cotton (yarn and manufactures) improved from Rs.75 corers to Rs.11,670 coreres.

Readymade garments —in recent years, the exports of cotton apparel or readymade garments have shown significant improvement. These exports were just Rs.9 corers in 1970-71. They jumped to Rs.196 in 1974-8-75. During 1998-99, cotton apparel exports touched a record of Rs. 18,700 corers. This indicates the increasing importance of this item in our exports.

Leather and leather manufactures - one of traditional items of Indian export" raw hides and skins. But recently, in the exports of this item, the proprprtion of leather and leather manufacture to raw hides and skins is on the increase. This is really a healthy development. India earned about Rs.39 corers in 1960-61 from this item. It touched Rs.486 corers in 1979-80 and rose further to Rs.6,956 corers during 1998-99.

Iron ore- India exports iron ore. India earned about Rs.30 corers per year from iron ore during g the First Plan. During 1970-71 exports of iron ore rose to Rs.117 corers and touched Rs.1,763 corers during 19998-99. This is an unhealthy development. India should increase the share of steel in exports by utilizing iron ore in her own steel plants.

Handicrafts- The exports of Indian handicrafts assumed great importance in the 1970's. From a low level of Rs.70 corers in 1970-71 they increased to Rs.120 corers in 1972-73 and stood at Rs.29,21 I corers in 1998-99. The most important items among the handicrafts were pear a precious stones which averaged Rs.3,177 corers during 1985-86 to 1989-90. at present, the single largest items of exports were of the order of Rs.29,211 corers out which gems and jewellery accounted for Rs.24,839 corers, carpets and works of art Rs.4,372 cores.

Machinery, transport and metal manufacturers

The expors in this category also include iron and steel, electronic goods and computer software. Even upto 1980-81, exports of this groups were a meager Rs.827 cores, but these exports started picking up and by 1990-91, they weer of the order of Rs.3,872 corers. During 1998-99, these exports have short up to Rs.18,580 corres, accounting for 13.1% of total exports. This is a com-mendable achievement.

Changing Structure of Exports

The structure of Indian exports is typical of developing economy. India has traditionally been an exporter of agricultural raw materials and manufacturers based on agriculrtural raw materials. There has been a contyinuous decline in the share of agricultural raw materraila and allied products. One reason for the relative decline of food, beverages and tobacco in the total exports is the increasing population and consequent increase in domestic consumption of these goods. Accordingly, the exports surplus in many traditional commodities like tea has not been increasing as much as the Government would have wished. In this connection, the growing importance of certain products in this category should be noted, i.e. fish and fish products, cashew kernels, coffee and rice. Vegetables and fruits also growing in importance.

Since 1960, under the impact of industrialization, exports of non-traditional items are gaining in importance. These items consist of engineering goods, handicrafts, which include pearls, precious and semi-precious stones and jewellery, iron and steel, iron-ore, chemicals, readymade garments fish and fish preparation. These goods constitute more than 50% of india's exports now. The fact, that some of these non-traditional items- such as engineering goods, handicrafts, readymades, etc.-have establkidshed themselves in the markets of even the most advanced countries shoews that they would continue to be poart of India;s excports in the years to come.

The sharp increse in the export of electronoc goods and software is a really welcomed development. The trend needs to be strengthened further. However, the export of some items id quite disturbing for the country- for instance, the export of iron ore and especially oiron and steel show the inability of the economy to use basic development goods. On the other hand, the import odf iron and steel is much more significant, showing the under-utilization of steel for capacity create in the country. Thus, the incressing contribution of non-traditional items in India's export efforts has been commendable but not consistent enough.

We should not, however, conclude that only non-traditional items are to the foreand the traditional items hace suffered a retreat. Exports of tradi-tional are also expanding, though probably not to the extent desire. Examples are the respectable growth in cotton fabrics, tea, leather and leather manufacturers etc.

Thus the pattern of india's exports indicates that

(a) the Indian economy is being diversified and (b) non-traditional items of exports are growing in importance.

(b) the large expansion of engineering goods is partly the relut of pick-up in demand in industrial countries wand also from the Middle-East countries whichhave under taken infrstructural projects like roads, ports and rai constructiuon, tele-communication and civil constructiuon

(c) India is now in a position to take advantage of both favorable demand situationand attractive price situation in international markets.

(d) While some commodities have tremendous exports potential (e.g. handicrafts, engineering goods and readymades). Other's (like sugar, jute, yarn and manufacturers, iron and steel) have fluctuated widely.

(e) With the announcement of the new agricututral policy, emphasis id being goven to boosting the export of agricultural produce. Rice exports is gaining importance. Besides this, fruita and vegetables an d processed foods are becomiomg significant ifn our exports.

Direction of India's Foreign Trade

In order to study the regional direction of India's foreign trade, it would be appropriate to classify the world in to four broad groupings; viz., America, Europe, Asia and Oceania and Africa.

So far as the American continent is concerned India had strong trade relation with North- America comprising USA. And Canada. Really speak-ing, USA is the dominant country in America. The countries of Latin America and other American countries, did not develop trade relation of much signifi-cance. Indicates that in 1951-52 India exported over 28% of her goods to America, out which 21 % o were sent to North America and 6% to Latin America. The share of Latin American countries declined over the years and they accounted for less than 1 % in 1979-80. The share of North America was 19% in 1969-70. But after the Bangladesh war in 1971, relation between India and the USA were strained and trade between the two countries declined. This explains to a great extent the fall in our exports to USA in the 1970's. During recent years, the positing has slightly improved and exports to USA were about 20% of total exports in 1997-98. On other side of imports, USA contributed 36% in 1951-52, its fell to 32% in 1960-61, rose to 40% in 1965-66, largely due to food grains imports, and was about 35% in 19969-70. As a reaction to the hostile attitude of USA, during the Bangladesh war India decided reduce her dependence on USA and thus imports from USA accounted for 10.4% of total imports in 1981-82. The share of USA in our imports has been declining over the years and was only 8.7% during 1998-99.

Historically, India had closed trade relation with U.K. It also had trade relation with other countries of Europe. For purpose of trade, the continent of Europe may be grouped under three broad regions; Western Europe, Eastern Europe and other European countries; Western Europe got divided in to two broad categories-the European Common Market, (ECM) and European Free Trade Area (EFTA).

In 1950-51, out of 31.5%og the total Indian imports from Europe 30.5% came from Western Europe. The share of Western Europe increased to 49% in 1955-56. Two factors were responsible for this; firstly imports from U.K. increased because she had to pay her sterling debt to India and secondly, the share of ECM countries more especially, West Germany increased sharply in our imports. Since U.K. decide to join ECM in 1973, the importance of EFTA coun-tries dwindled to barely 1.6% in our total imports. The share of ECM countries declined from 18.2% in 1955-

56 to 10.9% in 1969-70. However, part of the increase in the mere shift from the EFTA region. But if we take EFTA and ECM together, the share of European economic community (EEC) has been on the declined since 1955-56 and comedown to 21% in 1976-77. However, it improved to 24% in 1997-98.

Our trade with East European Socialist Countries viz., USSR, Poland, Rmania, Bul garia, Hungary, East Germany, Czechoslovakia and Yugoslavia developed in during the sixties. The main items of imports from these countries are iron and steel, non-ferrous materials, chaemicals, capital equipment, railway stores, paper, medicines and pharmaceuticals and petroleum poroducts. The imports of most of these commodities are of crucial help for our core projects and several industries of strategic importance. To these countries, in return , India exported tea, cashew kernels, tobacoo, oil seeds, leather , metallic ores, jute manufacturers etc.- the traditional items of Indian excports. The composition exports from these countries suggests the significance of the rade from the view point of economic development. In 1960-61, India imported 4% of her total imports from this region and exported about 8% of her total exports to this region. But soon after the Indo-Chinese conflict in 1962 and Indo-Pak war in 1965, our trade relation with the East European Socialist countries improved remarkably. In 1969-70 this group of countries accounted for 18% of total imports and about 22% of our exports. USSR as the chief contributor ac-counted for nearly 84% of trade with this region. By 1998-99, India's iomport from East European countries decline to 2% and our exports to these which declined to 14% in 1979-80 further fell to 3.2% in 1998-99. with the disintegration of the Soviet Union in to Common Wealth of Independent states(CIS), trade relation with thesecountries are under going a change.

Our trade with the countries in Asia and Oceania (other OECD countries) hfas been of grate significnce. Our export to these countries which were about 28% of total imports in 1951-52 increased to 32% in 1969-70 asagainst it, imports from these countries declined from 23% in 1951-52 to 19% in 1969-70. the ECAFE* region was of greate significance and two countries, viz., Japan and Australia were very important. Recently , Switzerland has become very important and its share in our total imports in 1998-99 was 6.9%.

However, due to increasing importance acquired by the imports of crude oil, OPEC countries have assumed very grete significance in our imports. These countries accounted for barely 8% in our total imports in 1970-71, but as against it their share in 1984-85 jumped to about 19%. Much of the increase was due to the sharp hike in the price of oil and did not indicate a corresponding increase in the quantity index of imports. On the ex[port front also our exports to OPEC countries increased from 6.4% in 1971-72 to 10.5% in 1998-99. with a fall in the international price of oil, the share of OPEC countries in our imports declined to 8.7% in 1986-87 but increased again to 18.7% in 1998-99.

The share of Japan and Australia in our exports that was about 15% in 1970-71 has come down-to 6.1% in 198-99. As against it, the share in our imports fro m these two countries has improved from 7.2% to 9.3% during the same period.

India has a great potential for increasing her foreign trade with Asian countries, because the Indian manufacturer are readily expectable in these countries. Similarly, India can export raw materials for her growing industries from these relatively more under-developed regions This evident by the fact that during 1998-99, imports this region accounted for 19.5% of our total imports areas they were in the range of 3.3% in 01970-71. on the export side, there has been a gradual and steady improvement and exports to this region increased from 10.8% during 1970-71 to a level of nearly 21% in, 198-99.

With Africa, our exports have remained, more or less constant to level about 6.7% during 1951-52 to 1970-71, but declined thereafter and stood at 5.3% in 1998-99. However, on the import front, the share of African countries has been fluctuating g from (% since 1951-52 but it has declined to low level of 7.1% in 1998-99.

Taking and overall view, it can be stated that India developed by the eightes or a more spatially dispersed pattern pattern foreign trade. It's excessive dependents on Western Europe and North America witnessed a gradual decline during the period 1951-52 to 1969-70 and there was shift in favor of East Euro-pean Socialist countries and Asian Counties, especially OPEC countries. But the during the eighties and the period of 1990-91 to 1998-99 which witness the disintegration of the Soviet Union into common wealth of independent states, the importance of Western Europe and North America have increased sharply. They together account for 58% of our export and 51% our imports in 1998-99 the share of Europe has dwindled to mere trickle and that developing country of Asia and Africa is increasing.

It would be of interest to examine the direction of trade with reference to some important countries,. USA, U.K., Germany, USSR, a-pan, Saudi Arabia, UAE and Switzerland, was the e8 countries of significance in our trade. The share of these 8 countries in our exports has declined from 57% to 47% during 1951-52 to 1997-98. As against it, their share in our imports has ranged between 45% to 46% during this period.

Although U.K. was of prime importance in our foreign trade before independence, USA was growing in importance up to 1970. During the seventies, especially after the Indo-Pak war of 1971. USSR grew in significance in our foreign trade. On the import side, the share of USA was the highest in 1998-99 followed by UK, Japan, Germany, and UAE. On the export side, India export to UK, were always higher than the exports to USA, but during the Third Plan the exports to USA, leveled off with exports to UK, and subsequently ex-ports to UK.fell further abnormally low level of about 6%. Our imports from Germany were on the increase till 1965-66, but have declined since then. As against it, our exports to this country have been of the order of 2-3% of total exports in the past but have risen 5.6% in 198-99. Japan is growing in importance in our foreign trade. We had trade relations with Japan in the pre-war period, but trade was cut off during the war. It has been revived again with USSR.

IS although our foreign trade is of recent origin, the share of imports was 2.5% in 1968-99 as against 0.2% in 1951-52. Similarly, the share of exports to USSR has risen from 1.0%-in 1951-52 to 21% in 1981-82 but declined to 2.5% in 198-99. With the disintegration of Soviet Union our trade with this region has suf-fered a serious setback. Iraq and Iran also become important especially for oil imports, but due to continued Iran-Iraq war, imports from these two countries become negligible but imports from Saudi Arabia rose to 4.5% and from Kuwait to 3.6% in 198-99.

Some salient features of the changes in the direction of trade in the post-Independence period may be noted here.

i) ***New trading partners***. Before independence, UK was the principle-trading partner for India, accounting for 34% of India's exports and 30% India's imports. After independence, even though India has continued to be a member of the British Common wealth, she has succeeded in getting new trading partners. Besides UK other countries of importance are USA, Germany, Japan a members of OPEC. Thus, an important feature of the new direction of the trade since 1951 is the increase in the number of trading partners for India. This spatial for geographical diversification of industries along with specialization in certain goods, and secure new markets for her products.

ii) ***Larger sources of imports***. The increase in the number of countries from whom we buy has been necessitated by many factors peculiar to the post-World War 11. For one thing, the planned economic development and the tremendous increase in the requirements for machinery, equipment, industrial raw materials, etc. could not be met by UK alone, or even by USA. for another, grant of aid and other assistance by international institutional institutions like the World Bank allowed India to buy from the cheapest sources (through global tenders). Thirdly, tied aid and grants some countries willing top help India in her planning effort necessitated India to import from particular countries, fourthly, foreign exchange shortage with reference to some capitalist countries. Finally, since the hike in the price of oil in 1973 India's imports from Iran, UAE, Kuwait, Saudi Arabia and other members of the OPEC have gone up.

iii) ***Larger and more attractive outlets for exports***. India has been diversifying her exports to much her imports. Naturally, she has to search for new countries to all her goods. Even though UK continues to buy a larger volume of goods from India, it has been relegated to second and even third place. USA has become the biggest buyer of Indian goods.

Likewise, Germany and Japan alone with USA and UK constitute the first four leading countries absorbing 37% o of India's exports. These are rich countries with high national and per capita incomes and they provide excellent markets for India's traditional goods (cotton and jute manufactures, specially carpet backing, leather manufactures) and non-traditional items such as marine product, pearls and precious stones, etc. Middle East countries offer a good market for Indian exports and account for 10% of our exports in 1998-99.

Scope for direction. The share of Africa and South America is only marginal. These are rich continents with very bright future. India should cultivate trade relations with-these countries- they could offer huge markets for India's exports. Likewise, the scope of India's exports to developing countries of the Middle East Asia is vast and in recent years, India is increasingly cultivating these markets.

The composition of imports by source reveals that OECD countries as a group accounted for the largest share in India's imports accounting for 51 in 1998-99. This was followed by the developing countries (excluding members of the OPEC) whose share was about 28%. OPEC and East European countries accounted for 18.7% and 2.0% respectively in India's imports in 198-99.

The destination-wise share of India's exports shows sufficient diversification. In 198-99, the share of exports going to industrial market economics as represented by OPEC groups was 58%, while East Europe and-developing countries accounted for 3%and 30% respectively. The countries of OPEC accounted for 10% of our total exports. during recent years, the share of countries of Asia and Pacific region in particular has been increasing in our exports.

CHAPTER-3

FOREIGN TRADE AND ECONOMIC GROWTH: AN A THEORETICAL STUDY

We have to go on and see what happens to two countries' trading relationships given economic growth. i.e. provided that some fundamental variables the trading system change. New methods will have to be used to do this. We then no longer study only the characteristics of a-static, never-changing situation. The methodology that we will use is that of comparative statics. We now start from a given equilibrium situation, introduce a change in one of the study the-implications for the new equilibrium, given this change.

Before we go into the theoretical aspects of economic growth the interna-tional trade, it is appropriate to say a few words about the long-run development of the world economy.

The Growth of World Trade during the Nineteenth and Twentieth centuries: A Bird's-Eyes View

The nineteenth century, form an economic point of view, is remarkable. Earlier centuries had witnessed economic development, but on a slow and mod-est scale. The limited amount of empirical evidence that exists show that, for instance in Great Britain, probably the most vigorously expanding country during the eighteenth century, total product grew by 5 per cent per decade from 1700 to 1780, and that income per capita increased by 2 per cent decade during the same period.

The shows that an economic transformation of the British society took place during the eighteenth century, and that the change occurred at a slow pace. The ninetheenth century, by contrast, showed very hight rates of growth in several fields. The growth of the British economic, for instance, was spectacular: Britain's population more than trebled during nineteenth century, despite heavy emigration and the national income seems to have increased more than seven fold at current prices.

Britain was not the-only country to experience rapid economic growth. The United states showed an even higher rate of growth, especially during the latter half of the nineteenth century. Several European countries overseas, too, especially those colonized by Britain, also showed rapid economic development.

The growth of world trade is an important aspect of economic development during the nineteenth century. The tables contain some important and interesting information. First, the rate of growth of world trade seems to have increased by about 10 per cent decade, or 1 per cent per annum.

Needless to say, the statistical information for this period is not too reliable. Trade between the relatively development countries and the more isolated parts of the world could possibly have been measured inadequately. Smuggling, Which at this time was not insignificant, is not taken into account, and so on. It is hardly probable, however, that factors such as these would influence the

Table: World foreign trade from 1750-1889

Approx.	1820 - 1850 -	1830 - 1860 -	1840 - 1870 -	1850 - 1888 -	1860 - 188-9	1870 -	1880 -	1750 -	1830 -	1840 -
World trade prices (millions of £)	153	315	410	662	1058	1616	2443	349	at 1865-85	
Rate of growth	10.1	30.2	61.5	59.8	52.7	53.7	43.4	Per decade (%)		

Source: S. Kuznets, Modern Economics Growth: Rate, Structure, and Spread; New Haven, Conn., Yale University Press, 1966. pp. 306-307

board tend, which shows that foreign trade at a very moderate pace the middle of the eighteenth centry up toapproximaty 1820.

After the Napoleonic wars, from around 1820, world started to grow at a brisk pace. During the 1820s and 1830s, trade speeded up, international trade growing at an astonishingly steady rate during most of the nineteeth century. The rate of growth, by roughly thirty year periods, was 50 per cent per decade between 1820-30 and 1850-60, and between 1850-60 and 1880-89.

The next thirty year, form the 1880s to the beginning of the First World War, also show a very marked increase in world trade, though the relative rate of growth was somewhat lower: form 1881-85 to 191-1-13, world trade grew at a rate of 37 per cent per decae. For the long period as a whole, i.e. form the 1820s to 1913, the rate of world trade was 46 per cent per decade.

Another interesting fact is the trend in foreing trade rations. We have seen that trade grew rapidly. For most countries, their foreigh trade grew faster than their national income. This led an increase in the foreigh trade quota. Around 1840, the proportion of foreign trade to the British national product was roughly 20 per cent ; at the outbreak of the First World War, this proportion had grown to over 40 per cent.[1]

Other European countris exprienced a similar development. The foreign trade proportion of France was 21.9 in 1859; around 1910 it had risen to 35.2. Italy and the Scandinavian countries also showed a market increase in their dependence on foreign trade. Germany is the only exception, showing a more or less stabe foreign trade quota during the later half of the nineteenthe century. Other 'new' countries which underwent a rapid economic

Table

World foreign trade from	1881- 1895	1913 - 1900	1881- 1905	1886- 1910	1891- 1913 -	1896- 1913	1901-	1906-	1911-	1885 - 1890
World trade at, 1913 prices (billions of $)	15.69	18.13	19.97	22.54	27.52	32.88	39.07	40.50		
Rate of growth	42.0	27.3	24.2	37.8	45.9	47.6	Per decade (%)			

Source: Kuznets, Modern Economics Growth, pp. 306-7

development showed a divers picture in the respect. Japan followed the general European pattern and had a rapidly growing foreigh trade ratio: Around 1880 it amounted to only 10 per cent of GNP; at the outbreak of the First World War it had risen to 30 per cent. Other 'new' countries, such as the United state, Canada and Australia, Showed a steady, or even falling, trade ratio. For Canada, the ratio showed some fluctuations, but the trend was on the whole steady. Australia and the United Sates showed a slight fall in their ratios: the United states had a foreign trade ratio of 13 per cent in the 1840; at the beginnig of the twentieth century, it had fallen to 11 per cent; apart from showing a declining trend, the foreign trade ratio of the United states was remarkably small.

In a general way, the changes in the foreign trade proportions could be redarded as the result of two competing sets of forces: on the one hand, those that induce growth o fdomestic output, and, on the other, those that induce growth of exports and imports. It is obvious that the trade-especially Britain, economically the most important, showed an export-biased type of growth. The major excetion is the United type of growth.[2]

To explain the pattern of growth and trade is a large and involved under-taking.

Nineteenth century was dominated by a great revolution in transport connected with the development of railroads and ocean transport. The railroads led ;;to an opening up of new territories such as the west of the United States, and of formerly underdeveloped part of Cannad, Argentian and Australia, which then become exporting areas of agricultural products. In Europe, the introduction of railroads led an increase in both foreign and domestic trade. The development of ocean trade between Europe and the countries overseas.

It seems that for the 'new' countries, such as the United States, Australia, Canada and Argentina, the improvements of transport had the strongest effects on domestic rtade. These countries also showed high ratres of growth during the nineteenthe centry. In Europe, on the other hand, improvements in transport mostly favored foreign trade.

Another important aspect was the continuous absorption of priviously closed areas into the network of world trade: Japan is the most conspicuous example. Apart form Japan and the 'new' countries referred to above, foreign trade did not induce any strong domestic grwoth. The other less developed countries remained underdeveloped and had mostly the character of trade posts of the developing countries.

Economic policy also played an important role. For most of the nineteenth ecntury. Britain was the world's leading economic nation. It was these the idustrial revolution started in the middle of the eighteenthe century, and consequently she become the center of the world economic. Britain was an island with limited re-Sources, so it was natural for her economy to be geared to trade. The classical in the early nineteenth century stressed, as we have seen, the gains and form trade. The doctrine of free trade. At least until the last quarter of the nineteenth century, there was also a marked lowering of trade barriers. This could hardly have done other than greatly favored the growth of world trade.

Britain's economic growth was centered around manufacturing. Ir was of an export-biased kind, and Britain was main supplier of industrial products to the rest of the world. As the British economy grw, it became increasingly specialized. it depended more on imports, of which agricultural goods and raw materials were the most important. Britain's imports came form the United States, to some extent from Central Europe, from what have been called 'regions of recent settlement' - i.e., Canada, Argentina, Uruguay, South Africa, Australia and New Zealand - and from the Scandinavian countries. All these countris experienced a great impetus for economic growth through an incrased demand from Britain for their exports. They coul start to grow by exporting food products and raw mate-rials to Britain, and they could continue to grow because Britain's demand for their exports kept growing.

A significant fact to bear in mind is that countries which could be classified among that less developed at this have - the regiouns of recent settle-ment and the Scandinavian countries - especially benefited from this type of growth. Table gives a hint of this.

Table: Percentage destribution of British imports by countries of origin

	1857-59	*1911-13*
United States	19	19
Other 'new' countries*	8	18
Industrial Europet	21	23
All other areas	100	100

*Canada. Argentina. South Africa, 6Australia and New Zealand.
*Germany, France, Italy, Belgium and the Netherlands.
Source: R. Nurkse, P atterns of Tede and Netherlands.

We know that Britain's imports grew rapidly during the inneteenthe Centuy. Table indicates that the 'new' countries increased their share of British imports very substantially. For these countries, and for some other, such as the Scendinavian countries, truly served as an engine of growth.

From the pint of view of theory, we can observe the following. We know that international trade along the lines of comparative advantage bring about an improved allocation of existing resources and gains from trade. But static trade theory has no implication for growth; it can only tell how resources ought to be allocated at a given point in time. At a time when transport improved greatly entered in efficiency, when policy barrier to trade were removed and countries entered into trade with each othter, static trade theory did have a great deal of releveance. But once the countries in question had started to trade and had reallo-cated their reraources, what happened?

On this, the static theory has little to say. What happened was that the central country of the world economy, Britain, grew at a steady pace. Her imports grew even faster. Her trading partners, the Peripheral countries' saw their exports expand rapidly; they could continue to grow along a pattern suggested by the theory of compatative advantage. The theroy itself did not promise any growth, but it all happened that the demand for the products in which the 'Peripheral' countries had specialozerd grew rapidly.

The first half of the twentieth century did not show any comparable expansion of world trade. Table illustrates that trade between countries continued to grow but on a much more modest scale. However, as a rapid increase in the growth of world trade took place during the 1950s and 1960s. This has meant that despite the marked lower rate of expansin of world trade during the first half of the centruy, the growth rate ofworld trade from 1913 to 1970 has been apporximately 37 per cent per decade or about 3.7 per cent per annum, i.e. only slightlylower, than that experienced during the nineteenth century. Indeed, if allowance is made for the First World

War, which was an abnormal period, the growth rate for the period 1928 to 1970 was 44 per cent, or almost identical to that of the period from 1820 to 1913.

Another important aspect of th develpment of world trade since the First Wrold War is its unevennesss. During the 1920s there was a modest growth of ound 1 per cent annum; in the 1930s there was a complete standstill. During the 1940s there was again a modest growth, and during the 1950 and 1960 a very rapid of growth.

Much of this development is explained by the upheavals of th first half of the twentieth century. During the sixty years since 1913, a full decade was taken up by the two world wars. Another decade wes characterizd by deep deprssion. Several years were taken up by the two world wars. Another decade was characterized by deep depression. Several years were taken up by recovery after the wars; these were painful years, especially for the countries that had suffered had heavy damage in the wars. On the other hand, the period since 1950 has been markedly free from disruption.

The development during the twentieth century has been characterized by two very different period. Trade increased at a slow pace among industrial coun-tries during the interwar period.

World wars impeded foreign trade more than output and the capacity to produce. The effects of the prolonged depression of the 1930s were also more harmful to trade than to domestic production; this was due to fact that the depres-Sion induced protectionist policies.

Since the beginning of the 1950s international trade has increased at a very Rapid rate. During a quarter of century leading up to the middle of the 1970s the volume of trade has expanded by around 8 per cent on an annual

Table

World foreing trade	1913 to 1974	1913	1928	1937	1950	1960	1970	1974
Index of volume	100	113	114	131	244	525	732	
of world exports (1913=100)								
Rate of growth per	8.5	1.0	11.3	86.0	115	(119)	decade(%).	

Source: Kuznets, Modern Economic Growth, p. 308.

basis. Production has also expanded at a rapid rate, but the increase of trade has out stripped that of production, and hence the degree of international interdependence has increased. The above description applies to many less developed countries, even though there are marked differences between various groups of countries.

Table: Foreign capital investments and the shares of three major countries before 1914 (absolute figures in biloions of dollars)

Gross foreign investment outstanding					
	Ca.	Ca.	Ca.	Ca.	Begin.
	1874	1880	1890	1900	1914
Great Britain	4.6	5.8	9.5	11.7	19.6
France	n.a	3.0	4.0	5.6	9.0
Germany	n.a.	1.2	2.8	3.4	5.6
Total	6.0	10.0	16.3	20.7	34.2
Volume per year,	1913	0.62	0.68	0.52	1.09
Total foreign investment, 1913 prices	4.9	8.6	15.4	20.6	35.3

Source: Kuznets, Modem Economics Growth, p. 322.

We have seen that world trade and trade among industrial countries in-creased at a relatively slow pace during the first half of the windiest century. This period of slow growth has been followed by two decades of rapid expansion in world trade. This pattern has also applied to the less developed countries in so far as the retardation of world trade was even more pronounced for them. How ever, they have not shared to the same extent in the rapid growth of world trade.

During the 1950s and 1960s. Will return to their situation and to the devel-opment of world trade since the second World War at the end of this chapter. First we will briefly examine capital movements and take a somewhat closer look at one case where trade functioned as an engine of growth along the standard nine-teenth-century pattern, the case of Sweden.

International Capital Movements

International capital movements played an important role during the ninteenth century. They provided an outlet for saving in the matured, industrial countries and helped to finance development in countries then emerging from a traditional, agricultural economy. They also helped to ease the balance-of-payments problems of the rapidly developing 'new' countries.

Table shows the position for only three major credit countries. These, how-ever, had a dominating position at the time : together, they accounted in 1913 for about three-quarters of the total gross debt outstanding. Table is therefore quite a good indicator of the amount and imporance of international a goos indicator of the amount and importance of international lending during the period in question.

The annual vallue of world trade in 1913 prices amounted in 1881-85 to avout $6 billion per year; it increased to about $13 billion per year in 1913. The capital outfows for the 1874-1914 period averaged between $0.5 and 1.1 billion per year. The outflowof foreign capital seems therefore have amounted to roughly 10 per cent of the trade volume. This is quite a substantial figure and shows that capital movements played an important role during the forty-five years before the First World War.

There was no marked rise in the annual flow of capital according to Table (with a possible exception of the last few years before 1914). Yet the increase in the coumulative

Table: Shares of debtor areas in outstanding gross investment in 1913-14(%)

Europe	28
United States and Canada	24
Oceania	5
Latin America	19
Asia and Africa	24

Source:Kuznets, Modern Economic Growth, p.322.

total of foreign capital invested was striking. The total amount invested rose from $4.9 to 35.3 billion (in 1913 prices) from 1874 to 1913-14. The growth rate per decade was 64 per cent, which is higher than the rates of growht of both foreign trade and national income. The explanation of the henomenon most have been that these foreign investments earend a good turn, and that these earnings were reinvested on the spot. On top of this came the net flow of capital frustrated in table. The result of this development was that the stock of foreign capital increased in relation to the national income. This applied to both lending and borrowing countries.

Most of these capital exports seem to have gone to fairly developed coun-tries. The available statistcs relate to 1913-14 only. Table shows the distribution of the outstanding foreign grooss investments at that time.

It shows that at least half of the foreign capital then outstanding had been invested in developed countries. Of the 28 per cent invested in Europe, most had invested in the developed parts of Europe. To this has to be added the United States, Canade and Oceania. Then the share going to these parts of the world is well over 50 per cent. If Argentina and Japanare also added, the share going to developed coutries increases to over 60 per cent.

It seems, however, as though the share of investments going to the less developed parts of the world could have risen during the period 1870-1913. It relatively, whereas investments in the less developed parts of the world - both in colonies and independent nations in Africa, Asia and Latin America - were on the increase. Figures for Britain seem to confirm thes view, as shown in Table 8.7.

Around the middle of the nuneteenth century and up to 1870, the bulk of British foreign investment went to Europe. During the latter part of the century and in the yeas leading up to the First World War, British capital went instead mostly to he 'new' countries, i.e. Argenntina, Canada, South Africa, Australia and New Zealand. It was investments in these countries the expanded by far the most rapidly. But there was also an increase, both absloutely and relatively, in capital going to the colonies; this was, after all the heyday of European inperialism.

Capital movements were substantial both in aboslute and relative terms during this period. The proportion of the annual outflow of capital to national output veried between 1 and 4 per cent for the mojor credit countries. During its peak periods, in 1880-89 and 1905-14, Britain sent 5 and 7 per cent, respectively, of its G.N.P. as capital exports was, of course, much higher. During the peak period it was close to 50 per cent, and during the whole period 1860-1913, between 25 and 40 per cent of gross domestic savings were invested abroad, a high figure indeed. Germany and France also exported a substantial share of their savings as capital exports aboad. These figure show tha the world economy had reached a high dergree of integration at this time.

Viewed from the angle of the debtor countries, these is little doubt that these capital imports played a critical role fo rspeeding up the rate of domestic investiment. The

United State had already at this time developed a high degree of autarky, but it still financed about 10 per cent of its capital formation by capital imports. Towards the end of the century, this position changed, however, and the United States, from being a debtor country, became a creditror a country, exporting capital, instead.

japan, the other large country that import capital, showed a more varied picture. During the time when it imported capital on a massive scale, from 1897 of 1906, it financed about 30 per cent of its domestic investment by imported capital.

Table: Foreign cepital investments since 1914, all countries (absolute figures in millions of dollars per year)

	1921 1929	***1930 1938***	***1921 1938***	***1951 1955***	***1956 1961***
Total per year, flows from all creditor countries	1547	706	421	4279	7145
Same flows, in 1913 prices in current prices (%)	1065	728	170	2038	3226
Great Britain	27.7	14.1	39.1	10.5	10.2
France	21.8	1.3	38.1	2.5	6.2
Germany	Net debtor			2.2	9.2
United State	43.0	78.1	13.6	78.4	67.4

Source: Kuznets, Modern Economic Growth, p. 323.

Capital imports played the largest role for a group of smaller countries. To this group. belonged primarly the 'region' of recent settlement', i.e. Canada, South Africa, Australia and New Zealand, the scandinavian countries, and Argenting. Canada, for intance, financed between 30 and 50 per cent of her investments by imported. Australia similarly, during the period from 1860 to 1900, financed be-tween 20 and 50 per cent of her domestic capital formation by imported capital. The bulk of Argentina's capital imports seem to have come during the first two decades of the twentieth century. During this perod, roughly 40 per cent of investments in Argentina were financed by foreign capital. The Scandinavian coun-tries had also substantial deficits in their balance of payments, which they fi-nanced by capital imports. During 1870-1910, foreign capital finanomic around 20 per cent of total investments in thes countires.

All these countries were 'Peripheral' with respect to the leading Eu-ropean industrial nagtions, especially Britain. Their exports to Britain and other mature industiral nations grew, as we have seen, very rapidly during this period. They needed to invest both in the traditional export lines and in various forms of social overhead capital to meet the increased demand for their export products. The original increase in deamand led to more ivestments which, in their trun, through a miultiipler effect, led to higher income and a still higher increase in demand, which led to more investments, and so on. The 'well-know accelerator-multiplier mechanism was at work guarnteeing growth. Slowdowns and crises occurred, but the over-all world economy grew rapidly, and world trade grew even faster. Then, as now, the less developed and semi-developed countries of the era needed capital to invest in order to grow. Being poor, they had difficulties in generating enough savings by themselves. To speed up their growth process they needed to import capital. We have just seen for severaof these 'Peripheral' cauntries both trade flows and capital formed an intergral part of theri growth process.

Capital movements played a very small role during the interwar period. This is illustrated in Table 8.8.

We know that the growth of world trade slowed down during the interwar period. The disruptiove effects on the international capital market ws even stronger. Before the First World War, a net flow of about $1. 1 billion went to debtor countries. During the period between the two world wars, olny a fraction-of this amount was invested abroad. During the 190s, capital movements still played a role that was not unimportant. During the 1930s, the net flows completely stopped; what happened was that capital was respatriated. During the interwar period as a whole, the importance of capital movements drastically diminished.

Since the Second World War capital movements have again been substntial. Howerver, they have of private capital flows geared by market considerations. The have to a large extent consisted of government grants and loans. About 30 per cent of capital export during this period has been in the form of goverments credit nation has been the United State. The Soviet Union and France have also been active in exporting capital.

Private capital flows, expecially in the form of direct investments, however have also played an important roll, especially in the years since 1955.

We can have a general understanding of the importance of trade and capi-tal movements, especially for the countries on the periphery during the nnineteenth century. Trade during this period functioned as an engine of growth for several countries. It might now be useful to illustrate this general principle by taking a brief look at how it worked in a specific case.

Growth and Trade During the Nineteenth Century: The Case of Sweden

Sweden was, in the beginning of the 1870s, a poorly developed country with more than 70 per cent of the population employed in agriculture. Certain prerequisites for growth were at hand: a compulsory school system had been introduced as early as 1842; the administration was honest and competent; and there was a tradition of manufacturing simple products from iron. Nevertheless, the country wa poor and primitive in many respects, and it would have been no great surprise if had remained so.

By the 1870s a sustained growth process had begun. The growth that took place was geared especially towards exports. The dominating export branch up to the beginning o fghe 1890s was timber and wood products, which made up around 35 per cent of total exports. Total exports expenaded fast ; the export volume rose, on the average, 4 per cent a year from 1870 to 1890. The terms of trade also showed a favorable development. Exports of timber and wood prod-ucts wents primarily to England, and the performance of Swedish exports during this period is a good example of how a country could grow by specializing in the production of raw materials that it sold in an expanding market at rising prices.

Another intersesting feature of Swedish exports during 1870-90 was the export of butter. This export group expanded most rapidly of all exports; it compried 20 per cent of the total in 1895. This reflects an important transforma-tion that took place in Swedish agriculture during this time.

Around 1850 Swedish agriculture produced mainly grain; of which it had a considerable export surplus. During the following decades Swedish grain ex-ports were outcompeted, especially by America and Russian producers. Swed-ish farmers turned instead to production of animal products , concentrating on butter , for which it found an expanding market in Britain. Some other of the traditional export branches , such as bar iron , were less lucky and underwent a drastic decline, especially in relative terms.

By the beginning of the 1890s a new export pattern emerged. Exports of timber and wood and agricultural products lost their momentum and were no longer focal in the growth process. New products took their place. For example, Swedish ironore deposits were rich in phosphorus. Technical progress in steel production (the application of the Thomas process) made it possible to extract the phosphorus from the iron . Thereby the rich ironore deposits in Lapland, in the north of Sweden, could be profitably mined. From the 1890s ironore became one of the expanding export branches.

Other export branches which built on the application of innovations were paper and pulp and engineering products. Innovations made it possible to use spruce and pine as raw material for the production of papetr and pulp. Swedish forests provided these trees in abundance, and paper and pulb and became one of the rapidly expanding export industries.

Swedish economic history shows many examples of unsucessful ventures in the enigneering industries during the latter part of the nineteenth century. By the end of the century the audacity and innovatie spirit of many Swedish enigneers and small entrepreneurs started to pay off, and somehighly successful companies began to exploit homemade innovations . Examples of such innovations were a lighthouse separators, diesel engines,some electric products, and, somewhat later, ball bearings. All this led to the engineering industry becoming one of the most expansive export industries from 1890.

At the outbreak of the First World War the new pattern of Swedish exports was firmly established. The shift in the structure of exports that began around 1890 had matured, and by 1913 the three most expansive exprort industires, iron-ore, paper and pulp, and engineering products, comprised roughly 40 per cent of total exports. This pattern has since continued with the engineering industry as the leading sector, so that over half of Swedish exports today consist of a well diversified list of engineering products.

Another very interesting aspect of Swedish economic development in the period from 1870 to 1913 is the role of capital movements. Sweden had, almost without exception, consistent deficits in her balance of payments during the forty from 1870 to 1910. There was only a short period from 1985 to 1897 during which Swedish trade balanced. The deficits were also quite large: they amounted, on the average, to between 15 and 20 per cent of total imports. This meant that a substantial part of Sweden's capital fromation during the countrty's transfor-mation from a less developed to an industrial economy was provided by foreigners. A large part of this external debt, incidentally, was paid off in inflated prices during the First World War.

This is an example of how, during the era of the classic gold standard,long-term capital movements on a large scale helped to invest, and also eased her balance-of-payments problems by providing much-needed foreign currency. According to the textbooks, the gold standard mechanism, given Sweden's strained blance-of-payments situation,should have forced the country to export gold and pursue a deflationary monetary policy. On the contrary, however, the capital im-ports led to an inflow of which in turn led to an increase in the money supply andmade possible an expansionary economic policy. A study of economic history could prove useful for those who are overly worried about the balance-of-payments problems of today's less developed countries.

Today's less developed countries seem faced with the more difficult problems. To grow by specializing according to comparative advantage and to concentrate on promoting export industries is, to many, a dubious proposition. Let us now look into the role of trade in the twentieth century.

World Trade Since 1945: The Less Developed Countries

We have seen that during the first half of the twentieth century, world trade grew at a slow rate. During the following twenty-five-year period from 1950, the growth of world trade had been strikingly rapid.

However, this rapid rate of development has been lopsided. Table shows that the expansion has been primarily concentrated on the exports of the industrial developed countries, the oil producers and a few less developed manufacturing countries.

The industrial countries have benefited from the rapid increase in world trade that has taken place during the last twenty-five years. For them, trade has grown faster than national income. Trade in manufactured products, especially, has expanded during the post-war period. Exports of these products have grown rapidly in many developed countries. This, in turn,has had a favorable effect on the growth of national income in these countries.

Most underdeveloped countries have not experienced a similar stimulus from trade. A few of the less developed countries have been able to show a rapid increase in exports of manufactured products. Among these countries are Mexico, South Korea, Hong Kong and Singapore. Table also shows that the oil-producing countries have experienced a very rapid expansion in the value of their exports. But the majority of less developed countries have continued to export traditional products, such as raw materials and agricultural products, demand for which has grown at only a relatively

Table: Growth and export shares, 1960-74
Average annual percentage growth rate of the volume of exports, 1960-74

	1960-5	*1965-70*	*1970-4*
(1) Developed market economy countries	8.6	11.6	10.0
(2) Developing countries			
OPEC producers	5.2	6.0	4.8
Fast-growing exports of manufactures	5.0	13.8	12.5
other developing countries	4.0	4.0	4.8

Percentage share of the world exports

	1960	1970	1974
(1) Developed market economy countries	66.8	71.9	65.5
(2) Developing countries			
OPEC producers	6.6	5.5	14.9
Fast-growing exports of manufactures	2.2	2.3	2.7
other developing countries	12.6	9.1	7.6
(3) Socialist countries Europe	10.1	9.9	7.9
Asia	1.6	0.8	0.7

Source: Unite Nations Conference on Trade and Developement (UNCTAD), Handbook for International Trade and Development Statistics, New York, Un-tied Nations, 1976, Sales No. Ef, 76. 11 D.32

Low rate. The result has been a continual fall in their share of world exports, as indicated in Tablc. The share of world exports of the less developed countries (disregarding the oil countries) was 25 per cent in 1950; in the middle of the 1970s it was down to roughly 10 per cent.

How fast the national incomes of the less-developed countries have ex-panded is a difficult question to answer in a precise and meaningful way. The paucity and

Table: Average annual percentage grwoth rate of real G.D.P. at market prices 1950-74.

	Total reat produce			*Per capita real produce*		
	1950-1960	*1960-1970*	*1970-1974*	*1950-1960*	*1960-1970*	*1970-1974*
Developed market economies	4.1	5.1	4.2	2.8	4.1	3.2
Developing countries	4.7	5.2	6.4	2.4	2.6	3.8
United States	3.2	4.5	3.7	1.5	3.5	2.7
E.E.C	5.0	4.6	3.9	4.3	3.9	3.2
Sweden	3.4	4.3	2.8	2.8	3.7	2.2
Latin America	5.2	5.5	6.6	2.2	2.6	3.7
Africa	4.5	4.7	5.2	2:3	2.0	3.5
South and South-east Asia	4.1	4.6	4.2	2.0	2.2	1.8

Source: UNCTAD, Handbook for International Trade and Development Statistics.

unreliability of data is one reaspn. The multitude ofless-developed countries and the lace of homogeneity among them should also be kept in mind when attempting generalizations.

Table covers only short period. If the information it contains can be taken at fae value, it says that national income grew at roughly the same rate for both industrial and less developed countries during the 1950s and 1960s. During the 1970s, and particularly following the energy crisis and the recession which it induced, real G.D.P. has tended to grow somewhat faster in the developing countries takne as a whole, i.e. including oil-producing countries. However, an energy-importing development area such as South-East Asia has experienced a fall in its growth rate compared with the previous decade. The difference in the growth of per capita income is primarily caused by differences in the growth of population. It also tells us that no 'pauperization' has taken place, at least not during the time in question: per capita income in the underdeveloped countries has grown, though at a modest rate.

The implication of the information contained in Tables however,is that trade hardly seems to have played any propulsive role for the growth in these countries. Expansion of trade seems at best to have kept pace with the growth in national income.

For several of the developing, 'peripheral' countries of nineteenth century, trad functioned , as we know, as an engine of growth. It seems that this has not been the case to anything like the same extent for the underdeveloped countries of today. Their difficulties in this respect seem to have started with the slowdown of growth of world trade that took place in the interwar period. Table 8.11 gives an indication of this.

A few of the less developed countries,especially those that happen to be oil producers, have done quite well, but the majorityu of them have seen their share of world exports fall. This is not only a recent phenomenon. It dates back to the 1920s. Then, less developed countries lost out at a time when world trade was stagnating,and they have been unable to recover their share at a time when trade has been rapidly expand. This development has resulted in the overwhelming share of trade today being, carried on between industrial coun-tries. This is illustrated by Table.

One important fact that must be kept in mind is that trade among themselves is most important for the industrial countries. When formulating trade policies,it is only natural for them to be primarily interested in measures that concern trade in industrial products,which to them is the most important part of their trade. Although their trade with lessw developed countries is by no means negligible, its value is less than one-third of intr-industrial trade. For the less developed countries, the reverse applies: for them, trade with industrial coun-tries is much more important than trade among themselves.

A complaint often voiced by representatives for the less developed coun-tries is that the terms of trade of these countries deteriorate. The terms of trade were defined as export prices divided by import prices. Not only has the vol-ume of exprots declined relatively, but the prices for the exports of the less developed countries have falledn relative to the prices they must pay for their imports.

It is not easy to give adequte measures of the development of the terms of trade for large groupsof countries. Differing results can usually be obtained depending upon what time periods are chosen,how countries are grouped,etc. It seems that the terms of trade

Table: Percentage share of developing countries in the value of world trade

	Including oil-exporting countries				*Excluding oil-exporting countries*			
	1928	***1950***	***1960***	***1974***	***1928***	***1950***	***1960***	***1974***
Exports	33.8	30.5	21.4	25.2	32.2	24.3	14.7	10.3
Imports	28.0	26.8	22.0	17.8	26.9	22.7	17.5	13.8

Sources: GATT, Trends is International Trade, Geneva, 1958; UNCTAD, Handbook for International Trade and Development Statistics.

went-against the less developed countries during the interwar period. The table shows that for the developed countries the period up until 1974 was one of the markedly stable terms of trade. The terms of trae of the developing countries improved during the 1960s.

During the 1970s the non-oil-exporting countries have experienced a decline in their teens of trade and this trend was reinforced by the substantial rise in the price of oil during 1973-4. The oil-exproducing countries, on the other hand, have had a termendous improvement in their terms of trade during the 1970s.

The export volume of the less develped countries has not been growing very fast,as we might expect that these countries would have been able to sell their exports at increasing prices, but that is not the case. The result is that trade has not transmitted growth. from the developed, industrial countries to the less developed countries the way it did in the nineteenth century. Income per capita has been growing quickly in the industrial countries, but it seems not to have led to a proportionla increase in the demand for primary products.

How are we to expalin this development? One answer has been suggested by Ragnar Nurkse. He gives the following six factors as reasons:

(1) The emphasis of industrial production in the advanced economies is shifting away from 'light' industries toward 'heavy' industries (such as engineering and chemicals) that is, from industries where the raw-material content of finished output is high to those where it is low.

(2) The share of services in the total output of advanced industrial coun-tries is rising, which tends to cause their raw-material demand to lag behind the rise in their national product.

Table: Total trade, 1974 ($ U.S., billions)

Destination	*World OPEC*	*Developed Europe*	*Developing market Asia Origin*	*O P E C countries*	*Non-Socialist developing*	*Socialist ecomomy*
World	845.350	595.940	34.720	137.130	62.960	8.320
Developed market Economy countries	542.520	398.610	29.000	84.760	21.130	5.560
OPEC	135.100	110.330	350	20.710	2.120	150
Non-OPEC developing countries	96.850	63.350	3.820	22.170	5.190	1.010
Socialist Europe	64.270	19.770	1.490	7.620	33.300	1.640
Socialist	5.950	2.700	165	1.900	1.190	

Source: UNCTAD, Handbook for International Tade and Development Statistics.

(3) The income elasticity of consumer demand for many agricultural commodities tends to be low.

(4) Agricultural protectionism has adversely affected imports of primary products.

Table: Term of trade (1970=100)

	Developed	*Other Developing*	*OPEC*
1960	96	97	98
1961	97	92	98
1962	98	93	100
1963	97	94	100
1964	97	99	102
1965	90	99	100
1966	98	105	104
1967	99	100	104
1968	99	103	104
1969	99	105	105
1970	100	100	100
1971	99	90	115
1972	100	90	113
1973	99	97	127
1974	87	96	337
1975	89	88	318

Source: UNCTAD, Handbook for International Trade and Development Sta-tistics.

(5) Substantial economics have been achieved in industrial uses of natural materials.

(6) Theleading industrial centers that the factors Nurkes refers toshould have played a role in causing the adverse demand conditions that many primary producing countries have faced during recent decades: The type of explanation that Nurkse

proposes, however, is not very systematic. It has too much the

character of being invented on the spot, of being ad hoc in nature We would like to depelop a more systematic framework for studying the effects of economic growth upon international trade. The is now waht we will set out to do. We will then be able to derive hypotheses to explain the development of the terms of trade. We will seek to state under what countries can be expected to develop favorably by trading and under what conditiions growth by trade will lead to an impasse.

A Model of Economic Growth and Internationa Trade Where Growth is Unspecified

The theory of economic growth and international trade, has been developed only in recent years.

Classical and neoclassical economists did not take much interest in the subject at least not in the theroretical aspects. The question of the long-run development of the terms of trade had alrady in the early nineteenth centruy been posed as a problem in economic policy. An exception was John Sturat Mill, when when he formulated the strikingly modern question 'What will be the effevt of technical progress in the export industries? But he devoted only one page to he the question in his Principles of Politiacal Economic and then went on to other fields.

As the starting-point for the modern theory of growth and trade, one can tum to a paper by J.R. Hicks published in 1953.

Hicks on Growth and Trade

The topic Hicks dealt in his paper was the long-run development of Great Britain's terms of trade and balance of trade. In the lalte 1940s and the early 1950s. Britain, like the rest of Western Europe, had experienced persistent deficits in her balance of trade. Hicks tried to explain these deficits with reference tc a change his reasoning of economic growth in the United States.

Hicks counched his said, that there are terms of the standard two-country trade same rate-the likelihood is that this there are two countries, A and B, and that only A growth, while B is stagnant. What will happen?

If productivity grows uniformaly in A - i.e. if all its industries expand at the same rate - the likelihood is that will benefit B. The simplest way to see this is to assume that money incomes rise to the full extent of the productivity increase in A, while incomes remain unchanged in B, because nothing has happened there. Then the cheapening of A's products would have been erased by the rise in incomes, and prices would remian unchanged in A. Prices would also remain unchaged in B, as nothing has happened there. Money income has not changed in B, so there is no reason why B should but a larger or smaller quantity of A's products than before. But A's income has risen and that will lead to an increase in demand of imports. This implies that the balance of trade will turn in B's fovor. To restore balance, the relative price of B's exports would increase, and she would get improved terms of trade. This would also mean an improvement in her real national income.

Naturally, the picture becomes more complicted if incomes in A do not rise at the same rate as productivity increases. In that case the outcome might be different. For the present we are only concerned with the main driift of the argument and will lay these complications aside.

The case in which productivity increases uniformly in all industries might be called the neurtal case. Let us go on and assume that the productivity increase instead is concentrated in th export sector and that we have what Hicks called an export-biased growth. What will happen then?

This case is extremely favorable for countryb. Suppose that incomes remain constant in both countries. The prices of B's exports will then remain constant, because nothing has happened in this counrty, whereas the prices of A's exports will fall. The terms of trade will, therefore, turn in favour of B. What happens to the volume of A's exports to B will depend mainly on demand conditions. If B's demand of A's exports is inelastic it might happen that the value of As exports would fall while the volume would increae. Under such circumstances As whole productivity gain might be exported away to B. Export-biased growth is clearly the type of growth that is most detrimental to A and most favorable to B.

But what if the productivity increases in A are concentrated in the import competing sector and A has import-biased growth? This is the case which is most favorable to A and least favorable to B, and can bve demostrated in the same manner as before. If incomes in both countries remain the same, the same import competing goods in A would have to fall. This would mean that a larger share of the market would be taken over by goods produced in A, because imports would be substituted with import-competing goods. The demand for export form B would therefore fall. This would deteriorate, and would be able to keeps all her productivity gains and on top of the improved terms of trade.

Hick's analysis provied a good start by giving a rough formulation of the problem, but his analysis is of a very tentative nature. It is difficult to see how the differnet factors he discusses hold together. Sometime Hicks argues in real terms, as for instance when he talks about the terms of trade, and other times in monetary terms, as when he talk about the balance of payments. How one is also very sketchy: the demand side, for instance; is virtually ignored. In order to come to grips with the problem of economic growth and international trade, we therefore have to go bey and Hicks's formulation and introduce a more formal kind of analysis.

A Model of Economic Growth and International Trade: The Basic Formula[2]

In order to study the effects of ecomic growth on international trade in a more through manner than, for instance, Hicks did, we have to use s more formal approach and set out a well-specified model: We can then derive a formula that in a neat way captures the effects of growth in two trading counties on insight into the interrelationships among critical variables in a general-equilibrium frame-work.

In the text of this chapter we will only set out the main formula discuss the assumptions and result of the model in a verbal way. The formal presentation of the model and the derivation of the principal result will be presented as an appendix to this chapter.

The argumet is set up in terms of the standard trade model, with two coun-tries and two goods. But countries porduce both goods so that specialization is incomplete. We know that economic growth occures, but at this stage we do not specifythe sources of it. The productive capacity of both countries increases.

Economic growth means that the productive capacity in one or both countries increases. this leads to an increase in the supply of one or both goods. But it also implies an increase in income. the increase in income will lead to an increase in demand.[3] The point is, however, that supply and demand of each good will not, in all likelihood, increase with the same amout. Therfore, relative price will have to change in order to clear the markets. If, for instance, supply of country I's export good increases more than the demand for it, there will be an excess supply of the good and its price will have to fall.

But a change in relative prices is, of course, nothing but a change in the terms of trade. The object of the model is to show how economic growth affects both the direction and the size of the changes in the terms of trade. We also know a great deal about its effects on the rational income.

It is now time to set out the basic formula that captures the captures the effects of economic growth in the two trading countries on their terms of trade. Before analyzing the model we will explain the notations briefly (exact definitions are given in the appendix). Figures in the subscripts stand for countries, x denotes export and m import magnitudes, C denotes consumption and S supply. Thus S_{1m} denotes supply (output) of the import -competing good in country I.S_{2x} stands for supply of the export good in the country II. C_{2x} denotes consump-tion of the imported good in the country I and C_{2x} denotes consumption of coup-try II's export good. Economic growth is symbolized by t. P_X is the price of country I's export good and Pin of its import good. Country I's terms of trade are given by P.($P=p_x/P_m$). It is obvious that country II's terms of trade are equal to I/ P.

R_{1m} denotes the growth rate of the import-competing sector in country I, and R_1 denotes the growth rate of the rational income in country I; R_{2x} and R_2 have analogous meanings. The four symbols e_1.e_2, s_l, and s_2 denotes demand and sup-ply elasticities. Country I's elasticity of demand for its import of impotables respect to the terms os trade of trade is given gy e_1, its elasticity of supply of imprtables with respect to Ps given by s_1, etc. E1m denotes the income elasticity of importabes in country I. E_{2x} stands for the income delasticity of exportables in country II.

An Analysis of the Model

That the outcome for the terms of trade depends on quite a number fo factors. The growth rate of the national incomes in the two countries are important. Which sector experience growth is also very imprtant. The development of demand, measured by income elasticitiees, also plays a role. These are the factors which have the stage, and they are depicted in the numerator.

The interrelationships between volumes and prices, measured by demand and supply elasticities,are important. They are depicted in the denominator.

The denominator will be positive provided that the two goods are substitutes (so-called 'gross substitutes') for each other in consumption in both countries. This hardly seems a very strong assumption to accept. The first elasticity, el, shows, as already stated, how demand for importables in countryy I changes if relative commodity pices change. If P increased, it would imply that the imported good had become relatively cheaper. Then we would expect consumers to buy more of the cheaper good (imoptables) and substitute this good for the other good (exportables) in consumption; if this happens, el will be positive.

Anologous reasoning can be applied to e2. This elasticity measures how demand for exportables in country 11 changes if the terms of trade change. If P would increase, it means that country II's changes if the terms deteriorate, i.e. The relative price of its exportables in country II increases. Then the sign of e2 is positive (see the appendix). The only assumption needed for this result is that the two goods are substitutes (gross substituties) for consumers in country II.

The other two elasticities in the demonontor are supply elasticities. the first one, s 1, shows how produiction of importables in country I changes as relative prices change. Let us say that P increases. This implies that relative price of importables falls. if the price of importables falls, its supply will also fall, because producers will transfer resources out of the sector. This means that sl will have a positive sign (for the exact defintion, see the appendix).

We assume in this markets. This competitive conditions prevail both in commodity and factor market. This implies that the production-possibility curve is concave to the origin. This means that producers are going of behave the way we expect them to behave, i. e. if the relative price of a good falls, they are never going to increase production of it.

If we are willing to accept the quite weak assumption of competitive conditions in production and gross substitutability in consumption, the denominator will be positive. The magnitudes of the elasticities which make up die demominator are very important for the adaptability of the two depend, on the factors depicted in the numerator. But just how much the terms of trade will have to change in order to get to a new equilibriums to be reached.

High values on the demand elasticity suggest that the two goods are easily substituted for each other in consumption. Any change in relative prices will therefore lead to a substantial change in quantities consumed. Analogously, high values on the supply elasticates also make for an easy adjustment. The higher the values on these elasticised also make for an and able the producers in the two countries are to change the pattern of production if relative prices change.

Generally speaking, we can say that the larger the value of the denominator, the smaller the change in the tenns of trade arising from any disturbance, and the easier the adjustment to price change by-producers and consumers in the two countries. Therefore, the elasticities in the denominator are very important, their values being a measure of the degree of the adaptability and the recollective capacity of the two trading economies. In the extreme case, when the values of the elasticities tend to infinity, the change in the terms of trade is negligible.

If the denominator m is positive, the outcome for the terms of trade de-rids on whether $R_{1m}\ S_{1m} - R_1\ E_{1m}\ C_{1m}$ >< $R_2E_{2x}\ C_{2x} - R_{2x}\ S_{2x}$. If the left side of this expression is larger than the right side the trems of trade will improve for country she will then find that some gains form improving-terms of trade will be added to her autonomous growth because of her participation in foreign trade. If the two sides are equal, the terms of trade will not change during the growth process.

The important factors are obviously the sectorial growth rates and the income elasticties in the two contries. In them are capturdd the effects of economic gorwth on supply and demand in the two countries. In order to emphasize the implications of let us for the sake of reasoning assume that country II is stationary and the counrty I is the only growing country. Then both R_2 and R_2 x are zero, and only the left part of the numetator in equation is of interest.

Given these assumptions, the reuslt for the terms of trade depends on whether the weighted growth rate of import procuction ($R_{1m}\ S_{1m}$) is larger or smaller than the weighted income elasticity of importables ($R_1\ E_{1m}\ C_{1m}$). If the former is larger than the latter, i,e. $R_{1m} S_{1m} > R_1 E_{1m} C_{1m}$, the terms of trade will improve for country I. Growth under these conditions will lead to an increase in the supply of importables which is larger than the increase in demand. This will create the markets, the price of importables has to fall, i.e. the terms of trade will improve. We can also think of this process as leading to a condition in which more of the home market for importables is captued by producers in country I. The demand for imports in country II find a decrease in demand for their exports. Therefore, they have to lower their pices in order to clear the markets; in other words, the terms of trade move in fovor of country I.

If it were the other way around, i e. if $R_1 E_{1m} C_{1m} > R_{1m} S_{1m}$, then the terms of trade would deteriotate for country 1, because in this event the demand for importables would grow faster than the supply of importagles. There would be an excess demand for impotables in country I at existing prices. The exporters in country II would find that demand for their product had increased; tp clear the markets the price of country II's exports would have to rise. In short, country I's terns of trade would deteriorate.

We can now compare these result with the ones suggested by Hicks. His reuslt lie in the same general direction, but because he never took demand factors into account, his analysis was, fonn a rigorous points of view, indetenninate. Hicks said that export-biased growth would turn the terms of trade against a country, and that import-biased growth would improve a country's terms of trade. With our terminology we interpret esport bias in Hick's sencse to mean that $R_1 x\ S_{1m} > R_{1m} S_{1m}$ and import bias to mean that $R_{1m} S_{1m} > R_1 x\ S_{1x}$. That is, we simply compare the weighted growth rates in the two sectors,and of the growth in the supply of exportagles is larger than the growth in th supply of importables, growth is said to be export-biased. If it is the other way around, growth is said to be port-biased.

It is, however, easy to see that Hicks's definitions of export and import bias do not necessarity imply a defnte change in the terns of trade. It is fully con-ceivable to have an export-biased growth in Hicks's senese and still have improvterms of trade. Couuntry I will get improving terns of trade if $R_{1m}\ S_{1m} > R_1\ E_{1m}\ C_{1m}$. Let us assume that the income elasticity of demand for importables, Elm, is equal to zero. As tong as there is any growth at all in the import-compet-ing sector, the teens of trade will always improve for country I. In such a case it is possible that Rlx $S_{1m} > R_{1m}\ S_{1m}$, or that the growth is export-biased in hicks's sense, and that the terns of trade will still improve for the country. This is explained by the simple fact that all the increased income caused by economic growth will be spent on exportables, and as tong as some growth occurs in th import-competing sector, economic growth will always give rise to an excess supply t of importables and to excess demand for exportables at existing prices. To clear the markets and reach a new equilibrium the relative price of imprtables will have to fall, i. e. the terns of trade wilt improve for the country.

If we would tike to use the notions of export bias and import bias and have a definite connection between bias and a change in the terms of trade, we will have to redefine the terms. if we define export biased growth as one in which the supply of exportables is incresed more than the demand for exportables, i. e. if $R_{1x}\ S_{1x} > R_1\ E_{1x}\ C_{1x}$, then export-biased import-biased growth will lead to deterio-rating terms of trade. Analogously, if we define import-baissed growth as $R_{1m}\ S_{1m} > R_1\ E_{1m}\ C_{1m}$, then import-biased growth will always imply imporving terms of trade.

Up to this point we have assumed country II to be stationary. If we instead assume that country I is stationary and that country II grows, exactly analogous result hold. Export-biased growth in country 11. i. e. R_{1x} S_{2x} > R_2 E_{2x} C_{2x}, Leads to a deterioration in her terms of trade, and import-biased growth, i. e. R_{1m} S_{2m} > R_2 E_{2m} C_{2m}, leads to an improvement in her terms of trade.

If both countries grow, the outcome for the terms of trade will depend on the type of growth which occurs. If both countries tend toward import-biased growth, i. e. if R_{1m} S_{1m} > R_1 E_{1m} C_{1m} and R_m E_{2m} C_{2m} > R_2 E_{2m} C_{2m}, the country with he greatest degree of import bias will get improving terms of trade. If both countries will have deteriorating terms of trade. if country I has an expot-biased growth and country II and import-biased one, the terms of tade will always turn against country I; the faster the growth rates and the larger the bias (regardless of country), the faster the terms of trade will deteriorate. This also holds, mutatis mutandis, for country II.

These are the kinds of result that can be obtained by model with unspecifield growth. Its strength lies in the fact that we, with the help of the modelm,are able to see the basic interrelationships between supply and demand factors in the growth proce. It is now possible to specify growth and see what the effects of increases in the factor endowments and of technical progress will be. Berfore doing this, however, we will say something about the effects of growth on the national income and touch briefly in some policy implications of the development of the terms of trade.

Growth, Trade, and National Income

If the growth rate of a country's national product is 3 per cent per annum if the terms of trade do not change, the country's national income will aslo increase by 3 per cent. If the growth is of such a kind as to make the terms of trade deteriorate, what might be called the 'autonomous' growth rate - the growth rate at pre-growth prices - will be higher than the realized growth rate because some of the growth will be exported away in the form of falling terms for trade. On the other hand, if growth is of a type to improve the terms of trade, the realilzed growth rate will be higher than the autonomous one, because of the home-generated growth, the country's real income will improve because of improving terms of trade.

Therfore, if one know something about how growth affects a country's terms of trade, one also knowns a great deal about its effect on noational income. Analogous to the method in treating the terms of trade, a formula can be derived ever, require a more elaborate formal analysis. We will therefore be content with 'some verbal commentary.

If a country has its growth possibilites confined to the exports sector, she might get adverse terms of trade. But this depends on the situation in the second country. If the second country also grows and if her income elasticity of demand for importables is high, demand for imports can be expected to grow quicky, and the first country is able to increase her exports at only slightly lower prices. In this way the first country can grow an deprosper by concentrating on increasing 'production of exports.

But if the second country does not grow, or if its income elsticity of demand for importables is low, the fist country might be in trouble. Under these conditons the demand for imports in the second country might incerease only slightly or not at all, and in order to sell an increased amount of exports the first V country will have to lower its prices, i. e. to acdept falling terms of trade. Now the prince elasticity of demand for importables in.the second country will be important. If this elasticity is low, it may be impossible for the first country to increase its revenue from exports. In such a case, growth by means of export is a dead-end.

The ultimat case on the pessimistic side is that of so-called 'impoverishing' or 'immiserzing' growth. This is the case on which a country ends up having a lower real income after growth because the loss due to deteriorating terms of trade has outweitghet the gain due to increased production.

The possibilty of impovershing growth was first contemplated by F.Y. Edgeworth, who upon reading John Stuart mill's analysis of theffects of improvements of production in export industries, drew the conclusion that under certain condition 'the exporting country is daminified by the improvement; and one good, all of which it expoted but did not cosnsume, and whereby each country im-ported all of the good which it consume,and whereby each conditions the foreign demand elasticity is all-inpotant, and the condition for impoverishing growth is simply that this elasticity be less than unity. If the first country grows and the second country is stationary, and if the foreign demand elasticity for the first country's exports is less than unity, total exports earnings will fall because of growth; and as the national income equals total export earnings, the country will become poorer because of growth.

If a loss specific model than the one Edgeworth had in mind is used, the probability of impoverising growth diminishes. Then production of importables has to decrease because of growth, or the sum of all elasticities which appear in the denominator in equation has to be less than unity.[7] These are both quite stringent conditions.

There is no reason toexpect the former to occur unless some non-reproducible factor is used tin the production of importables. The implocation of the sum of all the above-mentioned elasticities being less than unity is obviously that there are no possibiliteis of substitution, neither on the demand nor the supply side, in either of the trading economies.

Perhaps the case of impovershing growth should be viewed as a curiousity. But it brigs in focus the factors that may make growth through trade an impass for a country. This kind of growth improves the country's terms of trade, and her national income will increase by more than the autonomous growth. The favorable effects of import-biased growth will be reinforced if the country has a high in-come elasticity of demand of for her own export good and of the trading partner's economy has a low degree of adaptibility.

We have now seen of the basic factors that determine the effects on the national income of economic growth in open economies.

The Terms of Trade as a Policy Problem

The interested economists have shown in the long-run development of the terms of trade has alway been great, at times almost obsessive. One line of thought, inaugurated by the classical English economists, claimed that the development of the trade would be detrimental to the industrieal countries and benefit the primay-producing countreis. Keynes was a proponent of this school, and it has had its advocates even in our day. Another line of thought widely discussed during the 1950s and the 1960s is connected with the name of Singer and Prebisch. It claims that the development of the terms of trade for different reasons had, and would have, to be detrimental to the less developed, primary producing countries and beneficial to the industrial countries.

These various explanations for the development of the terms of trade have been both loose and intricate. It should be clear by now that type oftheorizing set forth in this chapter can generate hypotheses for the development of the terms of trade. We know that these hypotheses are internally consistent, because they have their foundation in a general-equilibrium type of theory. Because the theory on which they buuld is explicitly formulated, it is also easy to see what assumtions they rest on. It would be premature to evalute and criticize the therories men-tioned above now; this will have to wait until later, after we have dealt with the effects on the terms of trade of specified growth. But even at this point it should be clear that it is easy to set out a set of conditions which would lead to deterio-rating or, for that matter, improving teens of trade for a country.

A Formal Model of Economic Growth and International Trade

We will now set out the simple general-equililbrium model. It is a model with five equations in five unknowns (S_{1m}, S_{2x}, C_{1m}, C_{2x}, and p) and with an exogenous variable t. The model is rudimentary but it suffices for pedagogical purposes.[8]

The variables used in the model are as follows. Y_1 and Y_2 denote national income in counties I and II, respectively. S_{1m} denotes, as was stated in the text, output (supply) of the import-competing good in country I. S_{2m} stands for supply of the export good in country II C_{1m} denotes consumption of the imported good in country I and C_{2m} denotes consumption of country II's export good. Economic growth is symbolized by t. px is the price of country I's' export good and Pm of country I's import good. The import good of country I is used good and Pm of country equals 1. We then indicate country I's terms of trade by *P*.

We can then set out the following system of equation:

$$S_{1m} = S_{1m}\ (t.P(t)) \qquad 1$$

Equation shows that supply of country I's imports-competing good is a function of economic growth and of relative prices.

$$C_{1m} = C_{1m}\ (Y1(t),P(t)) \qquad 2$$

Equation 2 shows that consumption of importables in country I is a func-tion of its national income and of relative proces. Equation 2 is, in other words, a simple type of demand function.

We can then set out analogous functions for the second country.

$$S_{2x} = S_{2x})\ t,P(t)) \qquad 3$$

This equation illustrates that the output of exportables in country II is a function of economi grwoth and relative proces.

$$C_{2x} = C_{2x}\ (Y_2(t),P(t)) \qquad 4$$

Equation shows that consumption of exportables in country II is a function of its national income and of relative prices.

Finally, we have the following equilibrium condition:

$$S_{1m} + S_{2x} = C_{1m} + C_{2x} \qquad 5$$

Let us call coutry I's import good, good I Good I is thus also country II's export good, Euation simlply says that, in equilibrium, demand for good I must equal its supply.

We assume the above system of equaion to have a solution for t. By defferentiating the equilibrium condition, equation with respect to t we get:

Expression shows the effects of economic growth on the terms of trade. It might be convenient to rephrase it in terms of growth rates.

The growth rate of the import-compet ing sector at given terms of trade. The grwoth rate of the natinal income in country I. 'The income rate of the importables in country 1. The growth rate of the national income in country II. The income elasticity of exportables is in country II. The growth rate of the export sector for in country II at constant terms of trade.

Country I's elasticity of demand for its export good with respect to the trade. Country II's elasticity of demand for its export good with respect to the terms of trade. Country I's elasticity of supply of i mporables with respect to the tems of trade.

Country II's elasticity of supply of exportabale with respect to the terms of trade.

Increases in Factor Endowments and International Trade: The Rybczynski Theorem

As time went by both countries grew, but we did not tryto examine the causes of growth. In this chapter we will go a step further. Two factors of produc-tion, conventionally called labor and capital, will be introduced and we will study what happens to teh trading relatiionships of the two of the countries has an increase in the labor force or in stock of capital.

It will now suffice to take only one country explicitly into account, be-cause we already know the basic inter-relationships between the two countries, as expressed by the elasticity factor.

This theorn states that if one of the factors of production increases, the other one being constant, the output of the other good will decrease in absolute. We will then odd away with these assumptions and look into the general-equilibrium implications of the Rybczynski theorem. After having dealt with the effects on commodity ad factor prices, we will also give a verbal treatment of the effects of increases in factor endowments on some other factors in the trade model, especially on the national income.

The Rybczynski Theorm

We will make the by-now familiar assumptions that commodity and factor markets are characterized by competitive conditions and that the production functions are homogeneous of the first degree. These assumptions are necessary to establish our results. It is, however, not necessary to assume that procudtion functions are the same in two countries.

We begin by assuming that the two countries are trading and that country I is in the equilibrium.

It follows that the export good is labor-intensive and that the import-com-tin good is capital-intensive.

It might be useful to reiterate it in the following way. The assumption about constant commodity prices implies constant factor prices, which in turn implies constant labor/capital raios in the two industries. But how can we keep the two ratios constant when the amout of one of factors increase?

This can only be done by reallocating resources between the two lines of production. When the amount of labor increases, all the new labor has to go to the labor-intensive industry. To keep the old factor proportions, we have to release some capital from the capital-intensive industry and let it be combined with the new labor. But not only do we have to move some capital from the capital-intensive industry, we also have to move some workers from the capital-intensive to the labor-intensive industry. As long as the labor force keeps increasing, we have to move factors of production over from the capital-intensive to the labor-intensive line of production. This means that the production in the labor-intensive industry has to expand while production in the capital-intensive industry contracts. If this process were to continue indefinitely, the country would obviously become completely specialized.

But keeping commodity price constant is only a device for tracing the logic ofthe argument; it is hardly compatible with general equilibrium. It is nowtime to give up that assumption and to see what the implications are for all the important variables in the general-equilibrium framework.

Let us for the moment, however, ask the question: Under what conditions would point P' be a true general equilibrium point?

An increase in the labor force of Country I increases the productive capacity of the country and leads to an increase in the national income. In other words, an increase in income causes a fall in the demand of one of the goods. This implies, obviously, that the import good is an inferior good. P' can therefore be a possible equilibrium point only with the porvision that one of the goods is inferior.

We have now established thaht factor growth leads to a deterioration in the terms of trade for that good which uses the accumulating factor intensively. Because labour increased and the country's export good was the labor-intensively good, the terms of trade deteriorated for the country. Had the import-competing good instead been the labor-intensive good, the tems of trade would have moved in favor of the country, because in that event, assuming unchanged commodity prices, the output of importables would have increased and the output of exportables would have decreased. This would have created an excess demand for exportables at unchanged prices, and in order to clear the markets the relative price of exportables would have had to increase; i.e. the country's terms of trade would have improved.

We will now go on and make some remarks about some generalizations of the Rybczynski theorem.

Technical Progress and International Trade

Another perhaps more important element in modern economic life is technical progress. Innovations different kinds- technical progress, in short-have transformed the agricultural economies of the eighteenth century into the modern industrial economy. The study of the effects of technical progress on international trade needs no justification.

Again, classical and neoclassical economists showed no great interest in the study of the effects of technical progress. It is significant that many leading classical and neoclassical economists were so preoccupied with one type of factor growth - in increase in population for economic development.

We shall nowstudy how technical progress affects international trade.

The Classification of Technical Progress

We also assume the production function to be homogeneous of the first degree. Technical progress means that more output can be produced with a given amout of inputs-or, to use a different but equivalent formulation, that a given output can be produced with less inputs.

In the classification of technical progress we will, follow Hick's way of classifying technical progress. There technical progress is classified according to the effect it has on the marginal productivities of the factors of production. A neutral innovations is one which increases the marginal productivity of both factors of production in the same proportion. Labor-saving technical progress in-creases the marginal productivity of capital more than it increases the marginal productivity of labor. And capital-saving innovations increases the marginal productivity of labor more than they increase the marginal productivity of capital. Another way of viewing the effects of capital-saving innovation is to assume that the same capita/labor ratio prevails both before and after the innovation. Because the marginal productivity of labor has increased relatively, labor is now more attractive to the producers and they will try to hire more labor. As they do this its relative price goes up.

Neutral Technical Progress and the Terms of Trade

To study the effects of technical progress on trade we will again use the standard trade model, with two countries consuming and producing two goods and using two factors of production.

Let us assume that we have a country with two sectors manufacturing and agriculture. Manufacturing is the capital-intensive sector and agriculture is the labor-intensive sector. Manufacturing is supposed to be the innovating industry.

Producers in this sector will bid, therefore, at constant factor prices for more factors of production. Because the industry is capital-intensive they areespeically eager to attract more capital, and its relative price will go up. As capital becomes more expensive, producers in both sectors will try to substitute labor for capital in production, and the methods of production in both sectors will become more labor-intensive.

We can sum up the effects of neutral technical progress on the terms of trade as follows. Neutral technical progress in a country's export sector will always lead to a deterioration in the country's terms of trade, whereas neutral technical progress in a country's import-competeing sector will always give the country imporving terms of trade.

Thus the direction in the change of terms of trade caused by neutral technical progress is unambiguous. Just how much they will change depends on several factors. Demand factors are important. The lower the value of the income elasticity of demand for importables, the less the deterioration in the terms of trade in the unfavourable case and the more the improvement in the favour-able case. The explanation for this is that if the import elasticity is low, it implies that the increase in income caused by the innovation will primarily give rise to an increase in demand for exportables; this means, everything else being equal, that the export surplus at given terms of trade will be smaller in the unfavourable case and that the excess supply of importables, again at given terms of trade, will be larger in the favourable case.

The degree of adaptability of the two trading economicies, as measured by the supply and demand elasticities. The greater the degree of adaptability, i.e. the higher the values of these elasticities, the less change will be in the terms of trade.

We have now seen the effects of neutral technical progress. It is time to consider the effects of biased innovations.

Capital-Saving Technical Progress in the Capital-Intensive Industry

Hence, assuming constant commodity prices, capital-saving technical progress in manufactrue will lead to an absolute increase in output of manufactured goods and an absoluted decrease in the output of agricultural products.

Keeping commodity prices constant is just a device used to trace the through the argument. It ought to be easy now to see the implication for the new general-equilibrium situation. Technical progress leads to an increase in the national income and , if we disregard inferior goods, to an increase in demand for both goods. This implies that, at constant commodity prices, there will be an excess demand for agricultural goods, becaus demand for these goods has risen but supply to them has decreased. Hence the relative price of agricultural prod-ucts has to goup in order to clear the markets.

The implications for terms of trade are immediate. If manufactures are exported, the terms of trade will turn against the country; if they are imported, there will be an imporvement in the country's terms of trade.

To sum up, capital-saving technical progress in the export sector will always turn the terms of trade against the country when the export sector is the capital-intensive line of production. If, on the other hand, the capital-saving innovation occurs in the import-competing sector, which is the capital-intensive sector, the terms of trade will imporve for the country.

The effects of capital-saving technical progress in the capital-intensive line of production are thus unambiguous in the sense that se know in just what direction the terms of trade will change in the case of such an innovation.

But the amount of this change in terms of trade depends on several factors. Demand factors and the degree of adaptability in the two countries will play a role exactly analogous to the role they played in the case of neutral technical progress. The lower the income elasticity of demand for importables is in the innovating coun-try and the higher it is in the other country (assumed to be stationary), the better off the innovating country will be. The higher the degree of adaptability in the two contries, the less the terms of trade have to change in order to reach a new equilibrium.

We now have to treat the third and last possibility to be elaborated - that of labor-saving technical progress in the capital-intensive line of production.

Labor-Saving Technical Progress in the Capital-Intensive Industry

We assume that commodity prices are kept unchnaged and will try to infer the effects on outputs. To keep commodity prices fixed, factor prices will have to change, so capital becomes relatively more expensive. There are two reaons for this. The first is that as technical progress occurs in the manufacturing sector, costs are lowered and producers try to produce more to increase their profits. They will demand factors of production, and because the sector is capital-intensive, they are especially eager to get capital, the relative price of which will then be bid up. The second reason is that the innovation is labor-saving, which means that the efficiency of capital has increased relatively, and this gives rise in turn to a relative increase in the demand for capital and hence to a rise in its relative price.

The implication of this is that a labor-saving innovation in the capital-intensive sector can have any effect on relative prices. Contrary to what was the case with neutral and capital-saving technical progress in this sector, the effect on the terms of trade are indeterminate.

Let us now sum up the discussion of the effects of different types of technical progress on the terms of trade. Neutral technial progress-will always have a netative effect on the relative price of the good produced in the innovating sector. Neutral technical progress will improve a country's terms of trade if it takes place in the import-competing sector, and it will lead to a deteriortion in the terms of trade if it is confined to the export sector.

The effects of capital-saving innovations in the capital-intensive sector, and of labor-saving innovations in the labor-intensive sector, are also clear-cut. Again, relative commodity prices of the innovating product will fall. Hence if exportables are capital-intensive, and capital-saving technical progress takes place in this sector, the terms of trade will deteriorate for the country. Analogously, if the import-competing sector is labor-intensive sector and if labor-saving technical progress takes place within it, the terms of trade will improve for the country.

The effects of labor-saving innovations in the capital-intensive industry and of capital-saving innovations in the labor-intensive sector, finally, are indetenninte. The relative price of the innovating product might increase or it might decrease, but no specific conclusions can be drawn from a theoretical point of view.

One of the critical assumptions for the analysis has been the assumption that productio functions in the two sectors are homogeneous of the first degree. We learned, in Chapter 10, that this assumption was necessary for reaching quali-tative conclusions about the effects of factor growth on the terms of trade. It is, however, not a necessary assumption for reaching clear. cut results about the effects of technical progress. Here it is possibleto get results with more general, unspecified production functions. It is also easier to interpret these results in economic terms. It is necessary to assume that the production functions are lineraly homogeneously. A full-fledged mathematical exposition would take us outside the scope of the present work, so we will be content to give some verbal com-ments on the more general results.

Remarks on Technical Progress and the Terms of Trade with Unspecified Production Functions

Technical progress leads to a shift in the production function. With given inputs a larger output will be produced. As an analytic expression for a productioon function with technical progress we can write

$$Q= f(L, K,t) \qquad 1$$

where Q stands for output, L and K for labor and capital, respectively, and t signifies technical progress. The marginal productivities are mathematically represented by partial derivative of the production-function with respect to capi-tal and labor respectively. We can go on and take second partial derivatives, which show how the marignal productivity of labor changes.

In a similar fashion we can take partical derivatives with respect to t.[5] We can take ¶f /¶t, for instance. This paritial derivative describes the shift in the production function. It is a measure of the technical progress to the extent that it shows how much more can be produced with given inputs because of the technical progress. By definition, this partial derivative is always positive, because we take technical progress to mean an increased capacity to produce.

We can also take two other partial derivatives with tepect to *t*, $\P_2 f/\P L$, $\P t$ and $\P^2 f/\P k\ \P t$. The first shows the effects of technical progress on the marginal productivity of labor, and the second the effect of technical progress on the marginal productivity of capital.

These three partial derivatives are very important in determining the ef-fects of technical progress on the terms of trade and on other variables in the trade model. Once we know something about the sign of these derivatives, we also know a great deal about the effects of technical proress on the terms of trade. Other factors are, of course, also imprtant, but directionof change in the terms of trade.

Let us assume that we have technical progress only in the export sector. We know that this means that more exportables can be produced with given inputs, or, in other words, that $\P^2 f/\P t$ is positive. If technical progress has a positive effect on the marginal productivity of both factors of production, it means that both $\P^2 f/\P L\ \P t$ and $\P^2 f/\P k\ \P t$ are positive. This implies that the terms of trade will deteriorate for the country.

It is easy to understand why this must be so. Technical progress itself, symbolized by $\P^2 f/\P t$, will have a positive effect on output of exportables at constant prices, because more will be produced with given inputs. If the marginalproductivity of labor goes up because of the innovation, more labor will be attracted tothe sector and this will also havea positive effect on output. If the marginal productivity of capital increased by the technical progress, more capital will be attracted to the sector in an exactly analogous manner, and this will again have a positive effect on output. Hence all three factors will go in the same direction, and there will be an excess supply of exportables at constant fall; i.e. the terms of trae will trun against the country.

Technical progress in the import-competing sector. will have completely analogous effects, provided that both marginal productivities increase because of the innovation that case the three factors work in the same direction. More importables wil be produced at constant commodity prices. The country's own producer will capture a larger share of the market for importables. The demand for the other country's exports will fall,and in order to clear the markets, the price of the innovating country's improtables will fail i:e. its terms of trade will improve.

What is of importance, therefore, is the change in the absolute values of the marginal productivities. As long as the marginal productivity of a factor increases because of technical progtress, more of this factor will be attacted to the innovating sector from the non-innovating sector. The change in the absolute value of the marginal productivities, therefore, is what is important for the real-location of factors of production.

The Hicksian classification of technical progress concerned itself only with relative changes in the marginal porductivites. To understand Hicks's clas-sification we must take into consideration the fact that it was originally introduced to study the effects of technical progress on the income distribution. It is not difficult to understand that for the income distribution the relative change in marginal productivities is of prime importance. But for the effects on output, commodity prices, and allocation of factors of production, it is the absolute changes in the marginal Productivities that count.[6]

Hence as along as technical progress is of a kind which increase the mar-ginal productivity of both factors of production, the effects on output and relative prices are clear-cut. But there is no guarantee that innovations will have this effect. A *priori* it is possible that the marginal productivity of one, or perhaps both, factors of production will fall because of technical progress.[7] If this hap-pens, the result for the terms of trade is no longer determinate.

If, for instance, there is technical progress in the export sector, and if the innovation is of such a kind as to increase the marginal productivity of labor but decrease that of capital, we will have two forces pulling in opposite derection, At constant commodity and factor prices, labor will be attacted to this section, because the marginal productivity of labor is now above the going wage. This will tend to increase output of the good. At the same time, capital will be re-leased fonn the sector, because the marginal productivity of capital is below the going retrun to capital. This will have a negative influence on the output of the good. To this must be added the upward shift inf the production function itself, symbolized by $\P^2 f/\P t$. Which, of course, will always have a positive effect on the supply of the good. Hence there ate two positive effects and one negative effect on output of this kind of technical progress, and it is no longer possitble to infer anything about the effects on output relative prices.

We should now have afairly firm grasp of how technicla progress affects the terns of trade and output in the stanared trade model. Before we condulede this chapter in might be useful to comment upon how other factors, such as the national income and the income distribution, are afected by innovations. To derive formal experssion for these effects would ttke us outside the scope of this book. Aainst the background of this chapter it should, however, not be too diffeicult to grasp the main drift of the argument concerning the effect on these variables.

Technical Progress, The National Income and the Income Distribution

The effects on the real natoinal income are closely linked with those on the trems of trade. Technical progress which improves the terms of trade has a strongly positive effect on the growth of real income. With innovations that lead to deteriorating terms of trad, the case become more of the prospective gains in the growth of income.

If there is technical progress in the esport sector, and if this progress is of such a kind as to decrease or leave unchanged the marginal productivity factors of production, it is bound to have a positive effect on national income. But if the innovation (which is perhaps more likely) leads to an increase in the marginal productivities,a certain negative effect on real income will come from the export sector. This negative effect will play a larger role if the country's export share is large.

Technical progress in the import-competing sector, on the other hand, will always have positive effects on real income. Thus it is critical importance whether any progress occurs in the exportor in the import-competing sector.

The most favorable case one could construct in the would be that in which most technical progress would be concentrated in the import-competing industry and where any innovations in the export sector would be of a type which would lower th marginal production of the factors in that industry. Then which would lowe the marginal productivity of the factors in that industry. Then all the strategic variables, i e. the rise in the production functions and the change in the marginal productivities, would exert a positive influence on real income. In this case a large dependence on foreign trade would benefit the country. Especially it the two trading economies have small possibilities of reallocating resources and adapting demand to price change, so that the value of the elasticity factor would be low, technical progress of this kind would imply large in creases in the terms of trade for the innovation country and a fast growth of real income.

In the opposite case, that in which the innovations are concentrated to the export sector and the marginal productivity of labor and capital are rising sharply because of technical progress, the contributions to real income from the innova-tions might easily be dispersed through trade. The chances that this will occur are especially high if the export share of the economy is large and if the adaptability of the economy is low. Technical progress of this kind might lead to a situation in which impoverishing growth takes place.

Thus the same general factors which tend to increase the volume of importables and to give rise to improving terms of trade will also exert a strong positive influence on the growth of national income. Those factors, on the other hand, which increase the volume of exportables and make for deteriorating terms of innovations on real income to be comparatively weak. It should be stressed, however, that the effects depend to a large extent of the adaptability of the two economies, measured by the elasticities. If the value of the weighted sum of these elasticities is large, the terms of trade might be said to act as an excellent steering mechanism, and small changes in relative prices will give rise to rapid and efficient reactions from consumers and producers. In the terms of trade in-comes would be large. This should, however, not obsure the fact that it is ex-tremely useful to know which factors influence the terms of trade in the growth process. (To say that steering-wheel of a car might not move much during a trip is not to say that it is an unimportant part of the car.

Technical progress also affects factor rewards and income distrivution. If technical prgress is neutral, the effect on factor rewards depends on factor intensities in the innovating sector. If the industry is labor-intensive, neutral innovations will lead to a relative increase in the wage. If on the other hand, the sector is capital-intensive, neutral innovations will lead to an increase in the return to capital.

The effects of biased innovations are quite clear. Labor-saving technical progress will benefit capital, because it primarly increase the marginal produc-tivity of capital, and capital-saving progress will benefit labor, because it in-creases the marginal productivity of labor.

Capital-saving innovtions in the labor-intensive line of production are therefore the type of progress most beneficial to lab¯or. Analogously, labor-saving progress in the capital-intensive line of prodction should have the most favorable on the return to capital.

It is easy to see intuitively the economic meaning of these result. Capital saving innovations increase the marginal productivity of labor more than they do that of capital. This gives a stimulus to produces to use more labor, because it is now relatively more efficient. If the sector in which the innovation occurs is also labor-intensive, this will reinforece the demand for labor, so the wage be bid up even more than it would be otherwise.

Against this background it is easy to understand Wicksell's statement, to the effect that the capitalist is the friend tof the worker, whereas the innovator is not infrequently his enemy, at least in the short run. If the labor force is constant and capital accumulates, this is bound to have a positive influence on the real wage. In this sence, the capitalist-saver is the friend of the worker.

But certain types of innovations can easily have a negative effect on the real wage. A labor-saving innovation of a kind which would decrease the marginal productivity of labor, especilly of it were to occur in a capital-intensive line of production, could very well lead to a lowering of the wage. In this sense the good engineer might be an enemy of the worker.

Obviously, a good many cases of different effects of technical progress on income distribution can be constructed. We will satisfy ourselves for the peresent by merely pointing out those factors which will lead to a fast growth of the real wage.

If we also take factor growth into account, it is clear that if capital accu-mulates than the population grows, the real wage will increase faster than the real reant and the inocme distribution will trun in favor of labor. The higher the degree of captial-saving innovatios and thefaster the rate fo technical progress, the more the real wage will rise. This developments will be further increased if the innovations occur in the labor-intensive line of production and if the possi-bilities of substituting factors of production for each other are limited.

We should by now have certain insihgts into the thoretical aspects of economic gowth and international trade.

CHAPTER-4

POSITION OF FOREIGN TRADE OF INDIA DURING THE STUDY PERIOD

As we embarked on a period on a period of planning, during the fifties, import substitution came to constitute a major element of India's trade and industrial policies. Planners more or less chose to ignore the option of foreign trade as an engine of India's economic growth. This was primarily due to the highly pessimistic view taken on the potential for export earnings. A further impetus to the inward orientation was provided by the existence of a vast domestic market. In retrospect, it is now abundantly clear that the policy makers not only under-estimated the export possibilities but also the import intensity of the import substitution process itself. It has been as a consequence that India's share of total world exports declined from 1.91 per cent in 1950 to about 0.53 per cent in 1992.

The inward looking industrialization process did result in high rates of industrial growth between 1956 and 1966. However, several weaknesses of such a process of industrialization soon became evident, as inefficiencies crept into the system and the economy turned into an increasingly 'high-cost' one. Over a period of time this led to a 'technological lag' and also resulted in poor export performance.

In the meantime, some change in the attitude towards exports became perceptible. Several export promotion measures were put in place from the early 1960s. The 1966 devaluation, while not resulting in the expected improvement in trade deficit due to a combination of circumstances, brought out the problems stemming from an overvalued exchange rate. Neverthless, it will be correct to say that until the end of the 1970s, exports were primarily regarded as a source of foreign exchange rather than as an efficient means of allocating resources. Import substitution over a wide area remained the basic premise of the development strategy. The political Economy of the Foreign Exchange Regimes

The political economy of India's foreign trade and exchange control regimes before reforms were initiated in 1991 can be understood from the implications of its selective, discretionary, and non-market-oriented character. First, macroeconomic instruments, including most importantly the exchange rate of the rupee, were never used to address balance of payments problems except for the rupee devaluation of 1966. Given that QRs on imports were substantially below market demand, the domestic price of an imported commodity far exceeded its landed cost inclusive of tariff duties and other taxes. As such there were rents associated with a license to import. Thus the power to grant a license meant power to confer the right to the rent involved. Since the domestic price of an imported commodity, and hence the rent to be earned per unit of import, would depend on the total quantity of imports allowed in, the licensing authority not only conferred the right to the rent but also determined its amount.

It hardly requires much imagination to realize that if rents could be created and allocated, individuals and groups would spend resources in influencing their creation and allocation in their favour.

It should be evident even to a casual observer of the Indian scene that a significant amount of scarce talents and material resources that could have been used for producing goods and services were spent instead on seeking and dispensing rents. Senior bureaucrats who wielded power spent much of their time in meetings that decided individual cases rather than set broad policies. In a large country with an abysmal telephone system, businessmen from far corners of the country frequently flew to the seat of power at Delhi to influence decisions. Larger enterprises that had continuing business with the government maintained "embassies" in Delhi. Even if there had been no corruption resources spent on such activities would have resulted in significant deadweight losses since those resources generated no material output. But there was certainly alleged to be corruption ! Indeed, the point has been made that with a ban on corporate contributions to political parties, politicians gained resources for electoral campaigns through kickbacks from rents conferred. Of course, if adoption of favourable decisions and the prevention of unfavourable decisions had to be bought, so to speak, only those who could afford to pay the price would enter the market. Clearly entrepreneurs with relatively few material resources and contacts at crucial decision making agencies were unlikely to enter the market.

Foreign trade policy issues became the subject of intensive discussion in early eighties. It came to be realized that a scheme of import licensing under which imports were permitted only to the extent that domestic production fell short of domestic demand irrespective of difference in cost and prices, could only lead to inefficiency.

The view gained ground that a more liberal policy of imports of capital goods and technology would enable India to reap the benefits of international division of labour. The attempt therefore was to move away from import substitution per se towards efficient import substitution, so that considerations relating to cost and efficiency were incorporated in the overall policy framework. It also became increasingly clear that production for export could not be isolated from production for the home market and that trade policy had to be integrated with the policy for domestic industrialization.

While the signs of liberalized trade policy became visible in the latter half of eighties, it was only in 1991 that the country embraked on a truly liberalized trade policy with a short negative list of exports and imports and with quantitative controls over imports withdrawn for all, except consumer goods. It was recognized that trade, exchange rate and industrial policies must form part of an integrated policy framework if the aim was to improve the productivity and efficiency of the economic system.

A Decade of comfort

India's balance of payments remained comfortable during the Seventies. The adjustment to the first oil shock of 1973-74 was rendered smooth by a happy combination of buoyant exports, spurt in private transfer receipts and increased inflow of aid. Exports, benefited by the expansion in global trade, rose at an annual rate of 6.8 per cent in volume terms and by 15.6 per cent in US dollar-terms during the decade. An effective depreciation of the rupee occurred due to the link with Pound Sterling until 1973 and later, because of the lower growth in prices in India relative to other countries. Private transfers rose seven.-fold from $296 million in 1974-75 to $2175 million in 1979-80 and in fact, in the post first oil shock period, financed roughly 80 per cent of the trade deficit. Within two years of the shock, the current account balance turned into surplus and it was only in 1978-79 that a deficit of about 0.2 per cent of GDP appeared. The utilization of aid was significant and was substantially higher than the financing requirement for the decade, allowing for a build up of reserves. At the close of the decade the foreign exchange reserves stood at $7361 million providing cover for over 7 months of imports.

Balance of Payments upto 1981-82

The Period of *Difficulties*

During the eighties, issues relating to the balance of payments came to occupy the center stage in terms of India's macro-economic management. The impact of the second oil shock of 1979, the full effects of which spilled over into the eighties, was more severe than of the 1973-74. Between 1978-79 and 1981-82, imports almost doubled. The increase in POL imports accounted for a little over half the increase in the overall imports. This was followed by the second-round effects on non-POL imports. Export performance was depressed by the severe international recession of 1980-83 and recorded a volume growth of just a little over 3 per cent. Net invisible receipts continued to provide support to the balance of payments, largely ely in the form of earnings from tourism and the sustained buoyancy of private transfers. However, the sharp widening in the merchandise trade deficit resulted in a turnaround in the current account balance from a surplus in 1977-78 to a deficit in 1981-82 of the order of US $3,166 million or 1.8 per cent of GDP. Adjustment efforts considered essentially of an Extended Fund Facility (EFF) negotiated with the IMF, although there were also intensified efforts to improve domestic production of crude petroleum.

Balance of Payments during 1982-83 to 1984-85

Easing of Pressure

A reprieve came during the period 1982-83 to 1984-85, with the easing of pressure on the balance of payments mainly due to a decline in the volume growth of imports from an average rate of 11.0 per cent during 1978-82 to a little over 2 per cent. Net oil imports (net of crude oil exports which commenced in 1981-82 after the discovery of crude oil in Bombay High), declined substantially as domestic production spurted to 29.0 million tones by 1984-85. This indeed was the main cause of the easing of the balance of payments. Non-POL imports rose at an average rate of 3.6 per cent in dollar terms. Exports however, grew only at an average rate of 3.2 per cent, in volume terms, due to a combination of adverse internal and external conditions. The invisibles account deteriorated as the interest payments to service external borrowing acquired a steady rising trend. Private transfers stagnated with the arrest in the labour migration boom. As a result, invisibles including private transfers and other surpluses, which had financed 89 per cent of the trade deficit in 1978-79 could meet only 57 per cent of the trade deficit in 1984-85. The current account deficit fell to US $ 2,416 million or 1.2 per cent of GDP in 1984-85 and reserves, which were US $5,952 million at the end of the year, stood to cover a little over 4 months of imports. 29 per cent of the financing requirement of the first half of the eighties was met by the EFF. Commercial borrowings and non-resident deposits emerged as important sources of finance, meeting 21 per cent and 15 per cent respectively of the financing need. However, external assistance remained the major source of foreign capital inflows, accounting for 29 per cent of the financing requirement.

Balance of Payment During 1985-90

The Build up the Crists

The Second half of the eighties witnessed the building up of strains on the balance of payments. Current account deficits acquired a structural character, remaining at high levels throughout. Large trade deficits occurred year after year despite a robust growth in exports. Recovering from the stagnation in 1985-86, the volume growth of exports in the succeeding four years ranged between 10 to 12 per cent per annum on an average. The share of manufactured exports rose from 56 per cent in 1980-81 to 75 per cent in 1989-90. Imports in US dollar terms rose in every year of the period. The volume of net POL imports increases from 12.4 million tones in 1984-85 to 23.5 million tones in 1989-90. However, the fall in crude oil prices during the period helped to contain the oil import of foodgrains in 1988-89. Imports of capital goods rose by an average of 16.2 per cent during the period. Export-related imports as well as other miscellaneous imports also rose significantly. The category of non-DGCIS imports, comprising defence imports and imports of ships and aircrafts etc., also rose significantly from about US $1.2 billion in 1985-86 to US $ 3.1 billion by 1989-90. The support from invisible receipts fell in the face of steadily growing interest payments and the outgo on account of profits. Dividends, royalty, technical fees and professional fees. The current account deficit averaged $ 5.8 billion or 2.4 per cent of GDP during the period as against the Planning Commission's estimate of 1.6 per cent. The period also marked a deterioration in fiscal imbalances as the ratio of gross fiscal deficit to GDP rose from 6.3 per cent in the first half of the eighties to 8.2 per cent during 1985-90. Repurchases from the IMF under the EFF exacerbated the deterioration in the balance of payments. External assistance, commercial borrowing and non-resident deposits shared equi proportionally in the financing need. The result was a doubling of external debt and a rise in the debt service ration from 13.6 per cent in 1984-85 to 30.9 per cent in 1989-90.

The Crisis:, 1990-92

In 1991, India found itself in its worst balance of payments crisis since 1947. That there was a crisis in the making during the second half of 1980s had been evident for a long time. The inflow of foreign borrowing had increased at a rapid rate during the late 1980s. This was due to the excess domestic expenditure over income — the fiscal deficit of the Centre and the States soared to over 11 percent in 1991. During this period total public debt as a proportions of GNP doubled reaching the level of 60 per cent and foreign currency reserves were depleted rapidly.

Matters were made worse by an accompanying double-digit inflation in 1990-91. The oil price increase resulting from Iraq's invasion of Kuwait in August 1990 reinforced the crisis-like situation in India.

India's credit rating got downgraded as, for first time in its history. India was on the verge of defaulting on its international commitments and was denied access to external commercial credit markets. A net outflow of Non-Resident Indian (NRI) deposits commenced in October 1990 and continued during 1991. The only way left for India was to borrow against the security of its gold reserves transported abroad.

But something good emerged out of the BoP crisis of 1991- the long overdue economic reforms. Apart from an immediate programme of macroeconomic stabilisation, structural reforms were also introduced in the industrial and trade policy regimes with a view to improving the efficiency, productivity and international competitiveness of India's economy.

The overvalued exchange rate was corrected by devaluation in 1991, followed by partial convertibility of rupee in 1992-93 and then making the rupee fully convertible on trade account in 1993-94. Tariffs were also cut steeply to open Indian industry to foreign competition, The focus of import liberalization has primarily been on intermediate and capital goods industries with the imports' of consumer goods remaining, by and large, regulated.

The initial response of the economy, especially export, was very good, The years 1993-94 to 1995-96 were years of excellent economic performance with GDP having grown at 6.2 per cent in 1993-94 and by more than 7.5 per cent during 1994-95 and 1996-97. Exports grew by 19.7 per cent during 1993-94 to 1995-96.

The major reasons for such a high growth rate in exports were:

- World GDP grew by an average rate of 4.1 per cent per annum during 1994-97 compared with 2.4 per cent during 1990-1993.
- World trade (dollar terms) grew by an average rate of 9.8 per cent per annum during 1994-1997 compared with 6.0 per cent during 1990-1993.
- Imports of advanced countries (dollar terms) grew by an average rate of 11.5 per cent during 1994-1997 compared with 2.1. per cent during 1990-1993.

- Increase in India's share in world exports of its three major commodity groups, viz. Textiles, yarn and fabrics; pearls, precious and semi-precious stones; and clothing and accessories during 1994-96.
- Increase in the Index of comparative Advantage (ICA) of the above.
- Other export commodity groupOs in which India gained in terms of ICA during 1994-96 include fish and fish preparations; rice; coffee and substitutes; organic chemicals; footwear; and gold and silver jewellery.

However the boom was short-lived. Since 1996, India's export performance has been poor.

There could be several explanations for this. Firstly, there has been a major downturn in world trade since 1996, which has affected India's trade as well. Export growth has been further hampered by an appreciation of the real effective exchange rate in 1996-97 and 1997-98. This trend has, however, been reversed since 1998-99. There has as-been an adverse movement in terms of trade, which appears to have affected exports. Finally, there are the host of domestic factors - both policy related and administrative - which continue to hamper imports. These include infrastructure constraints, high transaction costs, SSI reservations, labour inflexibility, quality problems and quantitative restrictions on export of agricultural commodities.

However the surplus on invisibles has helped to reduce the deficit on the current account. Earnings from-invisibles have helped particularly during the critical years of 1996-97 and 1997-98 when the deficit on the trade account touched alarming levels close to $ 1.5 to 1.6 billion.

Trade Policy Reforms and Balance of Payments

The major reforms in policy introduced during the 1990s depict unilateral as well as multilateral characteristics. Unilateral reforms have been undertaken with regard to exchange rate policy, foreign investment, external borrowing, import licensing, custom tariffs and export subsidies. The multilateral aspect of India's trade policy reforms refers to India's commitments to WTO with regard to trade in goods and services, and trade related investment measures and intellectual property rights.

Exchange rate: The Macroeconomic stabilization and structural adjustment programme initiated in mid-1991 commenced with adjustment in the external value of rupee,. Which was determined on the basis of a weighted basket of currencies of India's major -trading partners. The rupee was overvalued for most of the period prior to 1991 thus adversely affecting exports. It has been estimated that the rupee was overvalued by about 30 per cent during the eighties (Gulati and Pursell, 1995). The rupee was devalued from Rs. 21 to Rs. 23.12 per US dollar on July 1, 1991 and to Rs. 25.95 per US dollar on July 3, 1991, amounting to a cumulative devaluation of about 19 per cent. This exchange ratecontinued till March 1992.

An explicit. dual exchange rate system was introduced in March 1992 on a temporary basis to facilitate shift to a more liberal exchange rate regime. The newly introduced Liberalised Exchange Rate Management System (LERMS) consisted of a free market rate along with an official rate set by the Reserve Bank of India (RBI) in US dollars. Forty per cent of current account receipts from exports of goods and services were to be surrendered at the official exchange rate while the remaining 60 per cent could be converted at the market exchange rate. Import transactions undertaken through the official rate included crude and diesel oil, kerosene, certain fertilizers, raw materials for fertilizers, life-saving drugs and imports by government departments. All other imports were to be undertaken at the free market rate. All capital account transactions, except IMF transactions, were undertaken at the free-market rate, RBI could intervence by entering the free market at its discretion to level excessive and erratic movements as well as to offset seasonal fluctuations in the exchange rate.

CHAPTER-5

FOREIGN TRADE POLICY OF INDIA

Trade policy of a country refered to the set of policy, which govern the external sector of its economy. In a developing country like India, trade policy is one of the many economic instruments, which is used to suit the requirement of economic growth. The twin objectives of India's trade have been to promote export and to restrict the level of import to the level of foreign exchange available to the govermnent. The basic problem for a developing country such as India happens to be the domestic non-availability of certain crucial inputs like industrial raw materials, machinery and technology. This bottleneck can be removed through imports. Higher is the rate of development; greater is the demand for imports. Though in the short run imports can be financed through foreign aid, in the long run imports must be financed by additional exports. The basic objective trade policy, therefore, revolves round the instrument and technique of export promotion and import management.

The importance of exports in the context of developmental planning was first recognizing during the middle of Second World War faced a virtual exhaustion. The genesis of the crisis of lay in the formulation of second plan strategy itself which placed great emphasis on the development of capital intensive industries in order to build upon the infrastructure of the economy. This necessitated a large volume of import, which in the absence of a corresponding increase in exports resulted in a several balance of payments crisis.

The policy of development through import subsitutation, which was followed in the second plan, requires a continuous increase in domestic investment. Whenever there is a short fall in the volume of investment, excess capacity occurs in the capital goods industries. This in fact, is one of the basic reasons why a large number of firms, which were primarily catering g to domestic requirement, where forced to look for export opportunities in order to improve their capacity utilization. The momentum for engineering goods exports really related from the domestic recession during 1967-69.

Since it was not possible to reduce the level of import beyond a certain limit, the need for earning more foreign exchange was imperative. The problem associated with generating additional export were primarily twofold:

(a) Some of the principle export items of India are primary products for which the price and income elasticity's of demand are low. This is true of products like tea, jute manufactures, lower quality cotton textile; etc. It was, therefore difficult to increase the volume of export of such items in any appreciable quantity. Side by side, introduction of synthetic substitute captured a part of the market, which hitherto was caters to by natural products. This was especially true of jute products, including carpet backing.

(b) With the increase in domestic incomes, the level of domestic absorption of mass consumption items increased. As a result the quantum of exportable surplus recorded a decline. This is true of item like edible oil, sugar; tea, etc. as a matter of fact, India turn into an importer of edible oils from the position of an exporter during planning period.

In view of above constraints, it was found necessary that any item that could be exported should be exported, i.e. conscious application of selectivity principle in line with comparative advantage was difficult to persue. It was also necessary to restrict domestic consumption to improve the ability of exportable surplus. The export policy Resolution that was passed parliament in 1970 stressed the need for restricting domestic consumption of certain items in order to generate adequate exportable surplus. This policy however, was revised in 1977 when the Janata party government came in to power.

Efforts were also made to increase the export of non - traditional items like engineering goods, chemicals, readymade garments, games and jeweler, etc, for which the overseas demand was high. Because of the relative advantage that the India manufactures enjoy due to low labor cost, it was possible to increase export of such items substantially, of course by extending necessary fiscal and financial support.

The government has also tried to change the composition of export - basket by increasing the export of higher value-added products. For example, India was traditionally a large exporter of semi- finished hides and skin but was a negligible exporter of finished lather and lather goods. The government, there for, decided to restrict the export of semi-finished higher and skin by imposing quota restrictions and also levying export duties. Simultaneously, fiscal assistance was extended to the export of finished leather and leather manufactures, a part from making the import of leather machinery easy for increasing the production capacity.

Inter se competition among union exporters in certain products groups each severe. Inter se competition generally involves lower price questions

being offered Indian exporters. This is of obviously is detrimental to national interest. Therefore, the government has to impose restrictions on the question, which might be offered by Indian exporters. This system is known as floor pricing i.e. a price is indicated for specific products below, which no Indian exporter can sell the same.

No country wants to perpetuate a system under which it will be dependent on another country for finding outlets its main export products or as course of supplies. One basic objective of trade policy, therefore, is to diversify the directional pattern of foreign trade. At the time of independence, India was mostly dependent on the UK, both as a market for her export products and as source of imports. As a deliberate policy measure, India has tried to forge new trade links with as many countries as possible. her Payments Agreements concluded with the Centrally Planned Economics played an important role in the directional diversification program. As a result, the dependence of India on any single country has considerably been reduced over the last three decades.

Export can play an important role in supplementing domestic demand, especially in times of recession. But even otherwise it was found that there many items whose production should be considerably increased but not sold domestically at remunerative prices as the size of the domestic market is not very large. Such items include carpets, handicrafts, gems and jewellery, etc. These items are essentially labor-intensive and therefore additional production such items would create new employment opportunities. But such production could be generated only if the additional production could be exported. India's export policy, therefore, tries to promote exports of such items with a view to generating additional employment in the economy.

However, export policy is not only concerned with export with promotion but it also has a regulatory aspect. At a time when domestic availability decreases necessary to impose limitations on the amount of exports. For example, in 1977 the domestic prices of tea increased considerably. To reduce the volume of exports, the government exports duty on tea, which made Indian tea slightly less competitive in foreign markets. This resulted in increased availability of tea in the domestic market through reduced exports. In 1983, exports of CTC were banned with the same objective in view. Another situation, which is just the reverse of the previous one, is there is an excess production in the domestic market resulting in the cash of the prices in the home market. In such a case, it is necessary for the government to find out export outlets for the increased production so that domestic prices can be maintained at a level, which will proper remuneration to the domestic producers.

The objectives of India's export policy can thus be summarized as follows:

(i) To earn adequate foreign exchange to finance the requires volume of imports;

(ii) to effect a change in the directional pattern with a view to reduce dependence on a single country/limited number of countries;

(iii) to supplement domestic demand for increasing employment opportunities;

(iv) to raise unit value realization by promoting exports of value added items;

(v) to impose minimum price regulation where *inter se* competition is severe; and

(vi) to impose controls when domestic availability is less than adequate.

Import Policy

The basic objectives of India's import had been to ensure that the limited amount of foreign exchange was properly utilized for her economic development. This meant that foreign exchange had to be allotted according to certain criteria. Those sectors, which were considered to be priority sectors, were allowed to import their requirements whereas imports of items, which were considered non-essentials, were either restricted or completely banned. By the end of the Third Plan, India had already developed considerable infra structural facilities and also developed a fairly large number of industries. Some it was found that capacity created in those industries could not be fully utilized because of the non-availability of critical imported items. The import policy therefore had to take care of their requirements so that the investment already made could make proper contribution to the growth economy.

Another basic objectives of import policy were to grant adequate protection to industries, which were being set-up. These industries being infant, would not be able to compet with the mature industries in the developed world unless some protection in terms of import policy, viz. tariff and/ or quantities restrictions, was extended.

To satisfy the above-mentioned objectives, to criteria were developed and followed by the Government. These are (a) indigenous non-availability and (b) essentiality. Tire First criterion means that if any item is being domestically manufactured or produced, import of that item will not be allowed. This policy obviously protects the domestic manufacturing units from overseas competition. The Second criterion, viz., essentiality, attempts to ration the available foreign exchange in terms of their contribution to plan priorities, i.e. only those will be allowed to be imported which are considered essential for the fulfillment of the plan objectives. Some liberalization was introduced in 1976 when there was substantial improvement in India's foreign exchange reserve position.

Another basic objective of import policy is to maintain do-mestic price stability. Wherever, there is a short fall in the domestic supplies prices would tend to move up. If imports are allowed, domestic supplies will increase, thereby preventing the rise in the domestic price level. However, it was not feasible to use the import policy to achieve this objective earlier as India did not have adequate foreign exchange reserves. After 1976, when the foreign exchange reserves position became comfortable, import policy was also used for domestic price maintenance. For example., the government spent considerable amount of foreign exchange on importing large quantities of edible oils during 1977-78 to prevent a sharp rise in the domestic prices of edible oils. It is clear weather import policy can be used to attained this objectives will depend on the amount of foreign exchange that the government can spare.

The objective of India's import policy can therefore the summarize as following.

i) to use the available foreign exchange according to national priorities

ii) to so allocate foreign exchange that capacity utilization is maximized.

iii) to creat protection to domestic industries; and

iv) to maintain price stability.

Alexander Committee Recommendations

Some changes were introduced in India's trade policy as a result of the recommendations of the Alexander Committee. The major recommendations of the committee were as follows:

1. In view of the changing domestic environment, the framework of trade policy should more development-oriented rather than control -oriented as in the past. There is a necessity to remove excessive controls, which characterized import policy in order to speed up the process of industrial development and for maximizing capacity utilization.
2. Importable should be classified in to three broad categories, viz., (a) raw materials and components, consumable, stores and spares (b) capital goods and equipments; and (c) consumer goods. The banned list should consist of the items which are either indigenously available or are not essential for domestic needs.
3. Tariffs should be used as the control mechanism rather than the import licensing system. In order to remove the uncertain which are associated with annual policy changes, import-export policy should be announced on a three-year basis.

In line with these recommendations, the import policy since then . has been substantially liberalized. So far as exports are concerned, the. basis thrust remains towards exports promotion subject to the restrictions, which might have to be imposed in order to take care of the domestic requirements. In line with the changes in the import policy export of many items was decanalised and only 57 items reexamined canalized through various government organizations. In order to ensure proper unit value realization minimum export prices were stipulated for a number of items.

Instruments of Commercial Policy

To implement the export import policies, a number of instruments are used by the government, principal among them being tariffs, quotas and licensing. So far as import tariff are concerned India's customs tariffs are broadly classified into four categories, viz., and 40%, 60%, and 75%, and 100%. Raw materials are generally placed in the lowest slab; imports of intermediate and capital goods are subject to the higher level of duty while non-essential items are subject to the highest rate of duty. These rates are subject to change according to ' the requirement of the domestic economy. But since India is a member of WTO, it is necessary seek waiver from the WTO before any increasing in the tariffs rates can be affected. If domestic situations so demands, government can exempt imports of particular items from the payment of customs duties or might reduced the duty leviable.so far as export duties are concerned, they are imposed on a small number of items. The basic rationale behind the imposition of export duty is to mop up windfall profits. Whenever, the Government finds that international prices are going up but there is no corresponding increased in the domestic pro-duction, it may decide to raise the level of export duty so as siphon off a part of excess profit from exporters. For example, export duties on coffee are changed quite often in line with the prevailing international prices. Beginning May 1985, export duty on coffee was revised eight times in three years to reached Rs.1,700 per tonne in May 1987. it was abolished with effect from August 26, 1998 when it was Rs.1.000 per tonne. This variation in the export duties can be very sub-stantial. As pointed out above, export duties may also be imposed to restrict exports in order to maintain domestic supplies, but it may not be possible levy such duties in definitely because international situation might changed. For example, Government of

India imposed export duty on tea in order to increases domestic availability. But subsequently it had to abolished the export duty in order to maintain the competitive strength of Indian tea in the international market

Another instrument which is used in quota. Quotas can be both for exports and imports. Imports quotas can be used not only to restrict the amount of total imports but also to change the resources of imports. For example, the Government may direst that import of specific items will be allowed only from the rupee payment countries, if item is not very essential. On the other hand, import of highly essential items may be allowed from any sources, i.e. rupee payment areas or the general currency areas. In India, quotas are operated through the licensing system. Most items to be imported require a license. The licenses issued are generally in terms of value. Export quotas used only when the volume of exports needs to be restricted for sake of domestic consumption. Export quo-tas are generally in terms of quantity.

Trade Strategy in the Sixth Plan

Trade policies need continuous monitoring and adjustment in line with domestic and international changes. Looking forward, the Draft Sixth Plan indicated the factors which preparing the medium term import strategy. These are;

(a) The import policy has got to be selectively; ibgera; in order to make the best use of the increasing foreign exchanges reserves. The case for such relaxation rests on three arguments: (i) to transform a part of the foreign exchange reserves into resources for development, (ii) to allow cheaper allow cheaper imports to stimulate competitive exports and reduce production costs in the domestic economy, and (iii) to provide an element of competition in certain sectors of the industrial system where efficiency may be suffering on account of excessive protection.

(b) The main thrust of the import policy would be to meet the requirements of the priority industries as well as export-oriented units.

(c) Imports needs of the units where no-availability of critical import inputs happens to be the cause of low utilization of capacity should be met.

(d) There is strong case to reduce the investment cost of new industries and, therefore, tariff rates applicable to imported capital goods and machinery should be selectively reduces.

(e) Where total domestic requirements are not as high as to make establishment of an industry on adequate scale an economically viable proposition, it would be better to import the items rather than getting them produced domestically. The pursuit of this policy will result not only in the better utilization of the existing foreign exchange reserves but also reduces domestic resource costs.

(f) There must be a well though out program for meeting contingencies especially in the field of essential mass consumption items.

(g) There should be a ban on non-essential consumer goods and those items the importation of which might adversely affect the growth of domestic industries, especially the small-scale units.

The Sixth Plan envisaged that both import substitution and export promotion would have to be accorded equal importance in view of the large projected deficits in the balance of payments. The major policy elements advocated were:

(a) The envisaged investment allocations during the Plan period should result in considerable degree of import substitution in industries such as steel, cement, fertilizers, crude oil and machinery and equipment. However, the policy for import substitution will have to be selective. The choice of sectors for import substitution should depend on the long-term comparative advantage. Even though it may be necessary, in respect of basic strategic sectors of the economy, for the Government itself to make such a choice, it should possible for the rest of the economy to leave the choice to be made on the basis of criteria of rates return.

(b) While following the policy of import substitution, it would be necessary to ensure that encouragement to import substitution does not in any adversely affect export promotion activities. Policies directed not to import substitution result in higher profitability for production for the home market an, therefore, unless remedial action is taken, there will be a pull towards domestic market and away from export markets.

(c) With respect to invisibles, incentives are to provide for encouraging inward remittances. Efforts will also have to make to invite investments from persons of Indian origin that are now residing abroad. There is also scope for expanding earnings from shipping, insurance and banking. The trade policy will have to be devised in a way, which will now allow such opportunities to be quickly available of.

(d) In the past the policy with regard to borrowings. in the international capital market was basically guided by the aim to keep the country's indebtedness within limits and to maintain the ability of debt servicing. It is now considered desirable to make selective use of the international capital market, especially for financing projects having high rates of return and also the capacity of generating exportable surplus.

(e) In view of the resources constraints, it would be necessary to limit budgetary export assistance to minimum. However, even with improvements in the import regime and other policy framework including price policy, it might still be necessary to provide some budgetary support in order to ensure that export performance is not adversely affected.

(f) The task of achieving the real growth rate of 9% per annum in exports will be easier if domestic inflation rate can be kept under control. The highest growth rate in exports in recent times was recorded during the two years when the rate inflation in India was much lower than that of rest of the world. The economic policy measures will, therefore, have to be directed to-the maintenance of the domestic price level, which will have beneficial effect on India's international competitiveness.

Trade Policy Changes Initiated Uring the 7th Plan

The Committee on Trade Policy, which was headed by Sri Abid Hussain former Commerce Secretary, submitted its recommendation in 1984.the Committee has suggested a detailed trade policy framework for the coming year. Some of the recommendations made by the Committee have since been implemented.The principal recommendations of the committee were as follows:

1. In an economy such as India, where export constitute 5 to 7 % of GNP, there is no possibilities of export-led growth. Indeed growth-led exports are the more likely scenarios in India.
2. Export promotion and import substitution are neither mutually exclusive nor alternative strategies of development. They represent two sides of the same coin. The policy mix should strike a balance between export promotions on the one hand and import substitution on the other. At the margin, however, there is a case for a preference in favor of the export sector.
3. Export production must constitute an integral part of production in the domestic economy. To begin with,

we would have to identify a few leading sectors where we can experiment with structural change and in the process, promote the cause o exports.

4. There is a clear nexus between trade policies, industrial policies and other economic policies. A complete solution cannot be found in the realm of trade policies alone; rationalization of other economic policies is also necessary. The object of this rationalization should be to increase the degree of competition in the economy and provide an environment where manufacturers would not only be under pressure would also have an incentive to bring about a reduction in costs.
5. Import liberalization, by itself, is neither a necessary nor a sufficient condition for stimulating competition and efficiency in the domestic economy. It would need to be used in conjunction with appropriate industrial and ecônomic policies increase competition within the economy, through a reduction in the degree of monopoly and a removal of barriers to entry by newfirms.
6. The present regime of export promotion policies is mostly a compensation for advantage faced by the exporters on account of domestic economic policies, and the element of incentive, if any, is very small.
7. The duty drawback system should be rationalized in such manner that it provides an expedition and complete reimbursement or taxes paid on inputs that enter into export production.
8. The regime of cash compensatory support must be maintained so the at the export sector is not at a disadvantage on account of either unrebated indirect taxes or the cascaded structure of taxation.
9. The present export replenishment system for export production should be reformulated along the lines of the advance licensing system for category of

manufacturer-exporters. Such import facilities should be duty free and subjected to the actual user condition. It should then be possible to eliminate licensing through the introduction of a passbook for each exporter. In effect, this would mean a permanent replenishment license for establishment manufacture-exporters.

10. The real effective exchange rate of the rupee should not be allowed to appreciate and should be maintained at a level considered appropriate for ensuring the competitiveness of exports.
11. Fiscal concessions are an important means of improving the relative profitability of exports. The Government may consider exempting 50% of the profits from exports from income tax.
12. It is suggested that export production, in appropriate cases, should be exempted from capacity licensing provision implicit in industrial policy and restrictions on imports of capital goods or technology in import policy.
13. Canalization of Imports should constitute the exception rather than the rule. In terms of economic criteria, it is clear that where the -size of imports is small or where there are variations in terms of differentiation and specification, the items should not as a rule is canalized. a-manufacturing firm should not be the agency for importing item it produces.
14. In the ultimate analysis, tariffs should replace quotas over time. The process on transition would have to be gradual as tariffs and quotas are not perfect substitutes for one another.
15. For the range of capital goods in the present restricted list, where the domestic production of such capital-foods, has been exsistencefor a long time, say, decade or more it would be advisable to de-escalate the level of protection in a planned manner.

16. There should be a rationalization of the tariff structure in the case of capital goods, which are ion OGL. Insofar as there is no domestic production °f such capital goods, tariffs are not needed as means of protection or as an instrument of trade policy. Imports of such capital goods should, in general, be subject to low tariffs.
17. The import licensing procedure for the residual category of capi-tal goods should be continued with some changes and rationalization.
18. At the present stage of our development, it is necessary to pro-vide a more liberal access to imports or technology in most sectors of the economy. In this context, it is important to distinguish between technology embodied in capital goods and disembodied technology in there form of know-how. The former should be governed by the import policy regime for capital goods. The Commit-tee would like to make the following recommendations approvis the latter:
    (i) In case where it is possible to buy foreign technology, without foreign equity constituting a part of the package, such imports should be placed on OGL subject to appropriate ceilings on lump sum payments and royalties for a specified maximum period.
    (ii) In cases where it is not possible to import technology without foreign equity participation, or where the ceilings mentioned above are exceeded, such imports should be selective and would need to be regulated by the Foreign Investment Board. These imports of technology should be permissible when there is guaranteed access to the continuous technological up gradation in the present firm, provided that the technology transfer are competitive and reasonable.
19. A high level protection for import competing industries cannot be justified for an unlimited period

of time, as it leads either to high cost or to monopoly profits or to both which are not in the interest of the economy in general and the consumer in particular.

20. In order to attain the objective of efficient import substitution, it is essential to de-escalate the level of protection and ensure that infant industries grow up over time and become competitive.

Long-Term Fiscal Policy

The Government of India has formulated a Long-term Fiscal Policy, which was presented in December 1985. The principal features of long-term Fiscal Policy (LTFP) relating to the foreign trade sector are a follows:

Reforms of Duty Drawback Scheme for Exports

The present scheme for duty drawbacks (of both excise and customs) for exports is somewhat cumbersome and leads to long delays in settlement of claims. Much of the complexity arises from having brand rates instead of a generally accepted rate for each industry as a whole.

It is proposed to drastically simplify the drawback scheme by eliminating the option of brand rates and operating the scheme solely on the basis of industry-wise rates. In order not to penalize export production or is intended to err on the side of generosity in assessing the average drawback rate that will be applied to each industry. Important advantages of industry-based drawbacks rates is that they benefit those firms, which economize on the use of dutiable inputs and penalize those do not.

Ad valorem Vs. Specific Duties

Economic analysis generally favours ad valorem rates of duty. But in, recent years, problems of evasion and related administered exigencies have lead to the replacement of some ad valorem rates by specific rates so that their revenue yields do not keep pace with inflation. In this way the existence or proliferation of specific rates duty tends to weaken the built-in revenue raising capacity of the tax structure. Recognizing that administrative consideration will call for continued levy of specific duties in many instances, it is proposed to institute a system where by all specific rates are periodically upwards keeping in view the price increase.

Restructuring of Customs Duties

The basic thrust of customs tariffs reforms will be to place increasing reliance on tariffs to regulate and progressively reduce the role of quantitative restrictions. The move in this directions should increase revenues, encourage less import-intensive forms of production, moderate the unjustifiably high protection granted by quantitative restrictions to certain industries and reduce the delays and uncertainties associated with the administration of import licens-ing. At the same time, tariffs need to be tailored to reduce the enormous multi-plicity o nominal a defective rates o protection conferred by the customs tariffs structure. The reformed tariff structure also has to balance the advantage of cost reducing pressure from import competition against the need for adequate levels for protection for domestic industry and the necessity to earn and ration scarce foreign exchange and the need for revenue.

In carrying out tariff rationalization it is important to distinguish between the following the broad categories of imports:

(a) Capital goods;

(b) Raw materials;

(c) Other intermediate goods (including components and so-called "universal intermediates"; and

(d) Non-essential consumer goods.

Further, in outlinining a desired tariffs structure for these categories of products, we must appreciate that in many cases the transition to the desired tariffs rates will have to be phased over several years to avoid undue disruption for domestic industry.

Ideally, in the long run there is as strong case for subjecting all capital goods raw materials, components and other intermediate products to the same rate of nominal tariff. This system, if it could be implemented, would have several important advantages. First, the substitution of present multiplication of the nominal tariff by a single rate would constitute an enormous simplification for both trade and industry as well as for the customs administration. Second, this would vastly reduce incentive for miss-classification of imports to evade taxes. Third, a single nominal rate of import duty would assure a uniform rate of effective protection (i.e. protection of value added) at different stages of production of intermediate and capital goods. This would encourage the economy to specialize in those activities in which it has competitive strength.

However, as a practical proposition, at our stage of industrial development, a uniform system of nominal tariff rates for capital goods, raw material, and component may not be immediately feasible. Since domestic industry has grown under different level of protection in the past and different industries have attained varying degrees of maturity, a uniform system of duties may involve excessive social costs in the medium term. It may, therefore, be necessary to provide for some differentials in rates of duty for imports, which are used at different stages of the manufacturing cycle. It is proposed to rationalize the customs tariffs in respect of intermediates, components, capital goods, and other finished products along the following lines:

(a) There will be a two-tier structure of customs duties for raw ma-terials and components. Thus, if the basic rates of components is set at X per cent, that on raw materials will generally be a somewhat lower Y per cent.

(b) For certain "universal intermediates" which are used in a large number of industries, the objective on reforms will be to move towards a rate of customs duty even lower than Y per cent. This reduction of customs duties will only be possible as a part of a package to lower cost of essential universal intermediates to Indian industry. Other elements of the package will include reduction of cost on indigenous production through increased efficiency. Where the universal intermediates are produced in the public sector, the Government will examined methods of reducing costs of writing off past capital investment. If, despite this program of cost reduction, indigenous industry is unable to compete at the proposed customs duty rate on universal intermediates, it maybe better to regulate competing imports through quantitative control (including canalization) rather than through unduly high tariffs, which have cumulative impact on the costs of production at subsequent stages.

(c) Capital goods which are subject to quantitative import restrictions will be taxed at the same rate as raw materials, that is, at Y per cent. Capital goods, which compete the domestic industry, but which are allowed to be freely imported, will be taxed at X percent.

(d) This structure will be introduced over a period of time after industry-wise examination. An industry-wise review will be undertaken to determine the list of industry where the above structure of duties can be implemented in 1986-87. in respect of other industries, a higher duty structure, with similar differentials, will be permitted. However, over a period of a few years, the higher duties will be reduced gradually to confirm to the normal pattren.this will proved sufficient time for industry to re-adjust and reduced domestic costs of production.

(e) For administrative ease, project imports will continue to constitute a separate category, subject to duty at a lower rate. The categories of project imports will, however, be progressively reduced.

(f) Tariffs for essential consumer goods, such as food; edible oils, life saving drugs and live saving medical equipment will continue to below or nil with vvolume of imports regulated through canalization procedure.

(g) Imports of non-essential consumer goods will continue to be banned.

(h) In the process of giving a greater role to tariffs in regulating imports, steps will be taken to ensure closer co-ordination between tariff policy and policies regarding import licensing.

A high-powered committee has been established in the Finance Ministry for harmonizing the tariff structure with related policies, particularly the policies of import and industrial licensing.

Thrust Commodities

To make the export promotion strategy more effective, the Government has introduced a concept of selectivity. It has identified 14 items as thrust Commodities as these enjoy high export potential. These are:

1. Tea, specially in packaged and value-added forms 2. Cereals in particular, wheat
3. Processed food, including fruits and juices, meat and meat products, and fresh fruits and vegetables.
4. Marine products, specially in value-added forms 5. Iron ore
6. Leather and leather manufactures, with an emphasis on the latter
7. Capital goods and consumer durables
8. Electronics goods and computer software
9. Basic chemicals
10. Fabrics, piece goods and made-up
11. Ready made garments
12. Woolen fabrics and knit ware
13. Projects and services

The planning commission has suggested more intensive promotional measures for these sectors.

Export Strategy based on Country-Commodity Matrix

The Government has formulated anew-comprehensive strategy identifying 15 major products and 15 countries which taken together account for bulk of India's exports. It is expected that if the trade and industry concentrate on these product-market configuration, the export marketing efforts will get more focused and out come beneficial.

The 15 items include gems and jewellery, cotton ready made garments and accessories, cotton yarn, fabric and made-ups; marine products, drugs and pharmaceuticals, transport equipment , metal manufacture, machinery and instruments, leather manufactures, synthetic fabrics and made-ups, oil mills, leather foot ware; dyes and intermediates, plastic linoleum products, and ready made garments made of synthetic fibers.

The countries which figure in the 15-15 matrix are the USA, Japan, Germany, the UK, Hong Kong, The UAE, Belgium, Italy, Russia, Singapore, Bangladesh, The Nether land, France, Saudi Arabia and Thailand. These countries are the major importers of Indian goods and the 15 products are the main foreign exchange earners. For example, these countries accounted for more than $ 20 billion out of India's total exports of $ 26.2 billion during 1994-95. out of this, $ 17.1 billion came from the 15 identified products.

The Ministry of Commerce has also chosen 10 countries as emerging markets. They are Australia, Brazil, Indonesia, Iran Israel, South Korea, Malaysia, Nigeria, South Africa, and Spain.

Similarly, fruits and vegetables, processed fruits and juices, processed minerals, sports goods, cosmetics and toiletries, woolen yam/fabrics/ made-ups, silk ready made garments, wool ready made garments, electronics goods and computer software have been identified as emerging products the exports prospects of which are bright.

About 200 exports facilitators are to be designated for focused export promotion. These facilitators will be responsible for taking steps to boost exports of that particular product for which they are designated. The major responsibility of the facilitated would be to prepare and supply to all the concerned exporters the database regarding the product group in the country, to facilitate visit of business delegation, to conduct market studies, to gauge consumer preference to co-ordinate participation in trade fares, and to identify and tackle tariff and non-tariff various beside solving other irritants.

A bilateral chamber of commerce or an export promotion council, also an individual or a company dealing in that product could be designated as facilitator.

Another important initiative taken by the Government was to set up a India brand Equity Fund in April 1996. The objective of the fund is to popularize the image of made in India product in overseas market. The Fund has the Government towards its cropus will contribute another Rs. 10 crore. The trust will then raise resources from the trade and industry and another sources to mobilise a total corpus of Rs.50 crore in 1996.

CHAPTER-6

EMPIRICAL VERIFICATION OF THE DATA CONCERNED

Macroeconomic Perspectives

The focus of this chapter is on the potential influence of excport promotion on ecoonomic growth, for a country such as India. Policies which target significant growth in exports, are often driven by th motivation to improve overall economic conditions. The views that export policy can be a catalyst of national economic growth received a major boost from the recent experiences of the East Asian nations. Even industrialized nations, such as USA, Japan and those of Western Europe, have been actively pursuing different types of export- subsidizations schemes over a considerable length of time. Time and again such policies are justified because they are likely to increase employment, national income investment and long-term economic growth. An interesting example is the 'National Export Strategy' report presented to the US congress in 1994 by the Trade Promotion Coordinating Committee, which repeatedly asserts that the export support programs are meant for a better US economy. The recent thrust of India's trade policy aims at a commendable, sustained long-run growth of exports. Hence, it becomes extremely important to identify the avenues through which growth in exports can increase the rate of growth for the economy as a whole. Before we get into a discussion of the Indian scenario, let us take a brief detour in seeing the availability analyses of exports in relation to economic growth.

In a significant paper, Michealy (1977) used simple rank correlation on a 41-country sample for 1950-73 to analyze whether the rate of growth of exports has been associated with GD, growth. In order to avoid spurious correlations, because export itself is a part of GDP, the rank correlation used 'export-share' as the crucial variable. Spearman's coefficient was significantly positive for the group as a whole. It was larger for a sub-sample of middle-income countries. Balassa (1987) found positive correlation between different measures of the rate of growth of exports and output growth. However, these studies did not address the casualty issue and there was no sound theoretical basis for these studies.

Feder (1983) used a neoclassical growth model to study the impact of export growth on the rate of growth GDP by hypothesizing a positive externality effect of export growth. This was captured by the inclusion of exports as an additional productive factor in the production function of the non-export sector. Then he used a sample of 31 semi-industrialized countries and found evidence of positive impact of exports on growth. Helleiner (1986) has strongly argued that a minimum level of development is required before the benefits of export promotion can be realized. A number of studies showed that the coefficient of export growth was significantly larger for the middle-income group. For poorer nations, the contributions of export growth in explaining growthin income have not been that significant. Kohli and Singh (1989) have investigated whether a 'minimum critical threshold' related to the trade structure itself, rather than income pre capita can distinguish countries. Using data on 41 countries, they have shown that the coefficient of export growth was significantly lager for the outward-oriented nations. Edwards (1993) nicely summarizes the findings of the existing literature:

> In sum, most studies have found that in GDP growth regression the importance and significance of the exports growth varies across groups of countries, causing some doubt on the desirability of pooling all these nations together in the econometric analysis. However, it is unlikely that this issue will be further evaluated until more sophisticated econometric techniques are used on pooled time-series-cross section data.

Theoretical papers dealing with the possible impact of export promotion on macroeconomic variables in a developing economy are scare, at least relative to the numerous empirical papers in this area. Much research is needed to isolate, and identify exact routes through which exports can provide stimulus to national income and employment. Feder (1989) focuses on supply-side issues. For example, it is the-supply-side link between exports and non-exports that leads to growth (Feder, 1989). On the other hand, earlier Keynesian models emphasized the role of export demand in generating higher output and employment in an excess-capacity economy. The question is, what theoretical framework befits the Indian experience - a question that is almost impossible to answer. A pure Keynesians framework does not allow for much price adjustment. Hence, the supply-side constraints operating on the export sector are entirely absent. Larger external demand always generates additional output and employment Structuralist macroeconomics often relates the rate of utilization to the degree of capacity utilization to give a 'long-run' flavor to the standard Keynes-Kalecki models. Hence, greater export demand, by increasing the degree of capacity utilization, would boost the growth rate. Whatever be the supply-side implication of export growth, one can't deny the beneficial effects of export growth on the traditional export products. Labor-intensive exportable may require a boost in demand to utilize unemployed human resources. Yet, the main focus of growth should be on the rate of investment, that is, whether an export bonanza can uplift the investment share so that the one-time impact is magnified through a second-round investment boom. A point that should be noted here is that the successful Asian exporting nation also exhibited significant savings investment proportion the GDP. In fact, a simple Keynesian model could be quite insightful for this purpose. Considering an economy with excess capacity where savings and im-ports are given in the following specifications:

$S = SY, \quad 0<s<1 \quad 1$

$M = my, \quad 0<m<1 \quad 2$

Exports are determined exogenously by the demand, worldwide

$x=X \quad 3$

Where investment demand function takes the following form

$I=\hat{I} \quad$ for $Y- Y \quad 4$

= á (Y). Y for Y > Y

á? > 0, á? < 0

Condition retains the basic feature of a simple Keynesian framework and modifies it by an accelerator relationship. Once *Y* goes beyond threshold level *Y*, investment demand starts responding to output.

Investment demand as is exhibit here is partially driven by 'animal spirit' and partially responds to actual output levels. We have assumed that the investment functions is concave in Y for $Y > Y$. There is no compelling reason for the assumption of concavity. In fact, if á was constant, we could guarantee stability by assuming $á < s + m$. Since we are dealing with a Keynesian framework, all the action is taken place away from and below the full capacity output level. If Y the full employment level of output, we are contemplating that as Y approaches Y, incentive to invest diminishes. For stability it is assumed that

$$á'(Y) \text{ at } (Y=Y) < s+m \qquad 5$$

We are now in a position to determine the equilibrium level of income Y which is given by

$$Y_e = I+X$$

Considering $Ye < Y$ and an increasing in X. It alters Ye by $(?X)/(s+m)$ provided the new Ye is also lower than Y. On the other hand, if $Ye > Y$, an increase in X would be responded to by a greater increase in Ye since the multiplier is changed to 1 /[s+m-á(.)]. This is fairly obvious because a boom in exports induces a second-round increase in the level of investment. This exposition talks about a 'one-time' movement rather than the entire growth path. The point is that if a rise in exports in a Keynesian system induces futher expansion in investments, demand output response would be much stronger. Therefore, the outcome is mainly dependent on the nature of investment function. If investment responds vigorously to capacity utilization only after the utilization reaches critical point, export expansion may have to traverse a long wav before it stimulates investment. To understand the relationship between export growth and growth in out-put one must start with the following basic relation ship:

$$Y = X+D \qquad 6$$

Where Y is GNP, X is the total exports and D is domestic demand or domestic component of aggregate demand, using to denote proportional change, one gets

$$Y = \ddot{e}X + (1-\ddot{e})\, D. \qquad 7$$

Where 0<ë<1, does not suggest any theory for determining the relation-ship between X and Y however, if one assumes that the aggregate X is entirely determined exogenously, which is usually done in a typical Keynesian frame-work, a growth in X would determine the other variables. Moreover, there has to be a positive relation between X and Y, provided the share of exports in GNP is positive,. The ideas are that an increase in X has a multiplier effect on Y. just a positive correlation between X and Y does not suggest that it would be signifi-cant. In fact, for export share to be very low an increase in X would have a negligible impact on Y But whatever it is in a Keynesian framework, it is impos-sible that X and Y would be negatively correlated.

In a supply-constrained economy, where Y is more or less determined from the supply side, Xand D would be inversely related. An increase in D will force X to come down and vice-versa. Just for argument's sake one can think of a situation where producers are quite reluctant to export and would concentrate only on the internal market. After the domestic market is saturated, they would sell the surplus in the global market. Hence, export would be determined as a residual. Growth of D would be negatively correlated with a growth in X, an if the share of exports in GNP is low, growth in Xand Y would be moving in opposite directions. As one can see, this is the exact opposite of the Keynesian model. Exports don't act as a driving force, but as a residual. Most of the empirical works in this area try to decide whether a significant relationship exists between growth in exports and growth in output, without really looking into the macroeconomic conditions that dictate such a relationship. We have just described two possible situations with a typical Keynesian and a non-Keynesian flavor. This has been done to reflect on the experience of the Indian economy prior to the initiation of the current reform process. We first present some empirical evidence in connection with export growth and GDP growth over forty years (1951-91) and then try to suggest an analytical argument which befits such evidence.

Empirical Evidence

We will utilize the data provided by the Economic Survey of the Govern-ment for India for the years 1951 to 1994 for the purpose. Let us first try to see the Granger casuality between the GDP at market price and exports at market price (all in Indian rupees). Although we have length, given th annual data series for the variables, we opted for a three period lag length for the test. We first tested the following relations:

i. $$\log GDP = a_0 + a_1 \log EXP(-1) + a_2 \log EXP(-2) + a_3 \log EXP(-3) + a_4 \log GDP(-1) + a_5 \log GDP(-2) + a_6 \log GDP(-3) + u$$

ii. $$\log EXP = b_0 + b_1 \log GDP(-1) + b_2 \log GDP(-2) + b_3 \log GDP(-3) + b_4 \log EXP(-1) + b_5 \log EXP(-2) + b_6 \log EXP(-3) + v$$

Then we have tested the standard zero restriction of

$$H_0\ (b_1 = b_2 = b_3 = 0)$$

and

$H_0\ (b_1 = b_2 = b_3 = 0)$. Following the F test we cnnot reject-teh first of the two Null hypothesis , although the second one is rejected at 10 per cent level of significance. Thus GDP Granger cause export but not vice-versa. Let us write the estimated regression equations by OLS as follows:

i. log*GDP*= -0.3274+0..0041 log*EXP*(-1)+0.2020**log*EXP* (-2) – 0.2698*log*EXP* (-3)+0.4997*log*GDP* (-1) + 0.2450log*GDP* (-2) +0.3411 **log*GDP (-3),* R^2 =0.9975, D.W.= 1-5712,F (6,34)=2250.4

ii. log*EXP*= -1.0645* + 0.2066log*GDP* (-!) +0.0373log*GDP* (-2) – 0.0061log*GDP* (-3) + 0.9269*log*EXP* (-1) – 0.0387**log*EXP* (-2) – 0.0717log*EXP* (-3), R^2 = 0.9968, D.W.= 2.0065, F (6,34)= 1736.0

Given the Granger causality, we decide to concentrate on th regressions involving export as the dependent variable and GDP s the explanatory variable. The above regressions clearly show that the GDP in different periods has different types of multiplier signs on export. A simple log linear regression of exports on GDP by OLS using data for 1951-94 yields an annually low D.W. statistic. The use of the Cohrane-Orcutt method yields significant results for first order autoregressive lag, with the following coefficients: logEXP = -4.2701 + 1.1087* logGDP-, R^2= 0.9921, D.W.=2.0742, F(2,40) = 2511.1. However, a co integration analysis with log of GDP as the independent variable explaining the log of export yields th following result:

Log EXP = -7.6855 = 1.5659 log GDP.

On the other hand, s we have clarified earlier, we cannot rely on the co integration analysis for the low power of the test. To make our analysis com-plete, a test of zero restriction on the coefficient of log GDP in the co integration regression rejected by the log-likelihood restriction chi-square test. So, a positive sign of the elasticity coefficient of the co integration regression clearly established a very strong positive effect of GDP on export.

However, the above results clearly state that exports did not have the effects on GDP as indicated by the Keynesian model. As will be discussed below, this exhibits some control or regulation as well as inertia on the par of the investor somewhere, which prevented physical investment from picking up in some response to higher exports. As a result, the major exports played the role of residuals, whereby domestic consumption of the product was given the priority and exports could be increased only when there was more production in than what the domestic market could absorb. The interesting point is that this happened in the aggregate not for any particular product or product group.

Non-existing of the Keynesian type multiplier in the context of the Indian economy is a major empirical result which corroborates the theoretical arguments advanced in this connection throughout the chapter.

In terms of theoretical relationship defined earlier, we have exhibited a negative relationship between X and Y as well as between X and Y for an economy which is supply-constrained. If we look back at our early conjecture, which suggest that fens in a protected market first satisfy their internal demand and then export the residua, it would fit the story in terms of the aggregate. But the anlyticaly, it is hard to compare a partial equilibrium outcome with the behavior of macroeconomic variables. It is quite logical to presume that there would be products for which export would be detennined by supply conditions and those, which depends on the state of the world market. In this sense Marjit and Sarkar (1995) probably look at one set of products. The other set would tend to act together to justify Keynesian conclusion. More demand would boost production and income. Yet, Y Granger causing X and not *vice-versa* matches the 'residual' theory, that is, a growth in GDP alone will lead to higher exports, leading to a situation of exports by 'compulsion' and not by 'choice'.

Another competing supply-side argument may be that it is a growth in X that reduces growth in D and hence the growth in Y because the export shares in GNP is fairly low. Unlike the other case, here the demand for our exports is inelastic, and serving the domestic market does not assume priority.

It has been argued time and again that India's large internal market does make the investment policies inward looking. With protection, such assize becomes even more lucrative. This is amply borne out by the fact that the new foreign investment proposals are pouring into cash in on the middle-and upper-middle-class market within the economy. As we have suggested, the residual role of exports at the industry level may find its match at the aggregative level also. Although a full fledge macroeconomic exercise is not done here, the benefit of doubt should go to a framework that gives prominence to internal de-mand. One should note that even in terms of supply side growth model as proposed by Robert Solow, the leading role of internal demand vis-a-vis exports couldn't be-necessary ascertained. The composition of internal and external demand does not affect even the off steady state growth rate, which entirely depends on the savings rate, rate of growth of population and technology. Growth of exports per se may not affect the overall growth rate significantly if the rates of savings and investment do not undergo major structural shifts. While comparing the Indian case with some of the successful exporting nations, it must be made clear that the 'Asian Tigers' have demonstrated phenomenal growth in the rate of the investment over the last twenty years or so, and have been able to maintain a very high proportion of GDP going into investments and savings.

Source: World Development Report, 1995 (The World Bank)

Between 1970 and 1993, all countries except India experienced a double-digit growth rate in exports. However, during the same period gross domestic investment for each of these nations expanded rapidly. In terms of Investment-GDP ratio or savings-GDP ratio, India has been lagging behind the other countries. It seems that higher growth exports leads to higher levels of real - output only when the complementary conditions of high investment/savings ratio to GP are fulfilled.

Many emprical study has been taken fmdout the relation between export & economic growth among these studies prominent are Emery's (1967), Michaely (1977), Heller (1978), Blassa (1978), Andelman (1984), and Chow (1987), These studies stablished very strong and positive between export and economic growth. The acknowled ged success outword oriented development in south korea, Taiwan, Singapore, and Hongcong etc. partial responsible for the moved towards markets based policies more over the developed countries recog-nised role of trade in promitting and industrial development how and middle countries as a result of this many developing countries have significantly libralised trade in the course there broad structural adjustment programmes. These reforms have benefited the countries taking them.

Foreign trade and economic growth in India during the last four decade followed the policy of industrialisation import substitution. The adoptimopinports substitution of strategies was development influence the con-sider of size factor and also because of export passmism. This laid to very inefficient domestic industries. The havey protection and subsidies to Industries be to exessive capital intensity and relatively labour absorption and thus generally aggrativating the unemployment and under employment problems. Nineteen 1990 ninthen one 1991 another policy has been followed the total openes index for India starts form 12.58 in 1900-1951 and 1991 it is 16.01.

Exports and Economic growth in India : 1950-1991

In order to evaluate the contribution of exports/imports in the economic growth we have run double-log-regression over time. The data-on exports and imports and gross domestic product have been teken from Economic Survey published by government of India. The data is in real terms. The functional from LNRGDP-f (LREXP) has been extimated over the period 1950-91. The regres-sion equation is

4.684 x 0.800 LREXP

t - statistics (14.06) (20.00)

Adj R^2	F-Value
0.91	400.20

The equation indicates a strong and positive relationship between exports (real) and GDP (real) and it is statistically significant the GDP (real) has been used as a proxy to economic growth.

Imports and Economic Growth in India (1950-91)

Similarly the contribution of imports to economic growth has been estimated by running a double log regression by using a time series data. All data is in real terms. The regression equation : LNRGDP = f(LRIMP) is as follows

			Adj R^2	F-value
	4.971	+ 0.712 LRIMP		
t- statistics	(11.43)	(14.66)	0.85	215.14

The result sthows a very 215.14 close relationship between imports and economic growth over the period under study. So, the empirical result clearly establish a very strong connection between in case of a very strong connection 'between in case of India solid can be concluded that foreign trade played an important role in economic growth of the country, despite the fact that govern-ment for a very long period ignored the export-promotion policy.

We have applied the multi-variate least square regression methods for analysing the exports and import time series. The data on exports/imports are in value rather than quantity terms, when as the theory of demand suggests that quantity is the appropriate dependent variable, therefore, we have deflated the value series by unit value index of exports/imports to obtain the proper dependent variable. Thus, the dependent variable has been obtained by

$$X \frac{VX}{PX} \text{.....................(i)}$$

Where, X = quantity of exports of some comodity class.

PX = Price of exports.

VX = Value of exports.

In specifying the export-demand function, we follow khan, 1974

Log X = bo+b1 Log (PX/PW) + b2 Log W+U + ... (ii)

Price and income elasticities are represented by b1 and b2 and bo is the constant term. We expect that $b < 0 : b2 > 0$

Similarly, we got the dependent variable for imports

M=VM/PM .... (i)

Where, M : quantity of imports of some commodity class.

PM = Price of imports.

VM = Value of imports.

After getting the quantities of exports and imports, by dividing their values with their respective unit value at constant price with 1980 as the base year, we estimated the elasticities by employing the functional form as suggested by learner and strerue (1970). The import demand function can be expressed as follows.

M=f (u/PY, PM/PY)...................... (ii)

Where,

M = the quantity of imports.

Y/PY = real income

PM/PY = the relative price of imports.

The least square regression has been run in terms of long-linear form:

Log M = log al + bl log y/PY + cl log PM/PY + log U...........(iii)

Since, we are estimating the important demand functions in logrith is; bl and cl are income and price elasticities respectively. The sign are expected to be bl <0; and cl >0

The result obtained by running all regressions on the data have been presented in the tables 31 and 42.

Estimation of income and price elasticities of exports of India : 1951-1994.

Table I presents the result of income elasticity and price elasticity of exports for the period 1951-1994. The result should be analysed with caution beause of the possibility of serial correlation as we have used the time series data. During thus period, the income elasticity of demand for exports of food and live animals, beverages & tobacco, crude materials excluding fuels, minerals fuels etc, Animal vegetables oil, fat, chemicals retailed prod. NE's Basic manufactures, machines transport, misc manufactured goods and total exports took the expected positive sign and it is significant. This confirms that globlisation of the Indian Economy with the rest of the world would be useful as there is sufficient foreign demand for Indian exports. Since, integration of the economy would make the economy cost efficient the demand for exports will increase more and thus India would be able to earn adequate foreign exchange in order to finance its import bill. As for as the price elasticity of demand for exports is concerned the coefficient took the unexpected positive sign in all cases. This shows that there are distortions in the various sectors of the economy which can be removed through liberalization and globlisat en:

Price elasticity and income elasticity of demand for exports of India according to SITC 1951-1994.

Table-1

Dependent variable	*CONST.*	*LNRGDP*	*ADJ R^2*	*F-VALUE*
Food Animal	0.86	0.228	0.38	9.47
Beverage & Tobaco	2.99	0.333	0.22	
Crude Material Excluding fuels	0.23	0.773	0.628	23.85
Mineral Fuels	0.58	-0.126	0.007	7.09
Animal Veg. Oil	0.16	-0.139	0.29	6.66
Chemical Retailed Prod. NE's	1.98	0.392	0.43	11.35
Basic Manufacture	2.99	0.152	0.39	9.87
Machines	4.36	1.016	0.79	54.98
Transport Goods	1.99	0.546	0.55	17.94
Total Exports	2.64	0.208		

Table-2

Dependent variable	*CONST.*	*LNRGDP*	*ADJ R^2*	*F-VALUE*
Food and live Animal	9.899	-0.677	0.02	1.345
Beverage and Tobacco	21.229	-2.196	0.49	14.436

Crude materials Excluding Fuel	-6.372	0:692	0.28	6.280
Mineral Fuels	-18.511	1.895	0.55	18.072
Animal Veg. oil, fat	-58.318	5.062	0.80	54.988
Chemicals Related Prod.	-20.956	1.997	0.78	49.747.
Basic Manufacture	-12.076	1.251	0.40	10.203
Machines,Transport	-0.164	0.255	0.002	0.963
Misc. Manufactured Goods	-13.837	1.236	0.241	5.304
Total Imports	-6.181	0.915	0.64	25.326

Estimation of income and price elasticities of imports of India : 1951-1994.

Table 2 presents the income and price elasticities of imports of India for the period 1951-1994. The income elasticity of demand for imports took the expected positive sign in all the cases. This implies that with increase innational income, imports will go up as revealed by the international trade theory. There-fore the best policy is to liberalise the imports as they also act as a critical input for most of our exports. The price-elasticity of demand for imports took the expected negative sign in all the cases. But it is not significant statiscally.

The careful analysis of these tables reveal that Indian economy does have the necessary attributes for the success of market mechanism and recent changes in the trade policy in an attempt to liberate and intergate it with the rest of the world, would prove fruitful and productive. Some more data after these policy changes, is required.

This establishes that foreign trade plays an important role in economic development in India. The income elasticity of demand for exports/imports of India is greater than one and sufficiently high. This emphasized the need for globlisation of the Indian economy.

The price elasticity of demand for exports/imports is also important but not always. But in some cases, it is statistically significant. This implies that Market-Mechanism can be helpful and made operative in India. For this more liberalised trade policy is needed. Hence, we feel strongly that recent steps taken by the government towards globlisation and libralisation would yield productive results.

CHAPTER-7

SUGGESTION AND CONCLUSION

Foreign trade has worked as an *'engine of growth'* in the past (witness Great Britain in the 19th century and japan in the 20th, besides others), and even in more recent times the "outward-oriented growth strtegy" adopted by the Newly Industrialising Economies of Asia, viz., Hong Kong, (now a special administered area of China), Singapore, Taiwan, malaysia, Thailand, and south korea, has enabled them to overcome the constraints of small resource-poor under-developed economies.

Contribution of foreign trade to Economic Development Foreign trade contributes to economic development in a number of ways.

The primary function of foreign trade is to explore means of procuring imports of capital goods, without which no process of development can start. It provides for flow of technology which allows for increases in total factor productivity, and some short-run multiplier effects for countries with unemployed labour.

It generates pressure for dynamic change through (i) competitive pressure from imports, (ii) pressure of competing for export markets, and (iii) a better allocation of resources.

Exports allow fuller utlisation of capacity, increased exploitation of economies of scale, separation of production patterns from domestic demand, and increading familiarity with absorption of new technologies.

These, in turn, help increase the profitability of the domestic business without any corresponding increase in price.

Foreign trade increases most worker's welfare. It does so at least in four ways: (i) larger exports translate into higher wages; (ii) because workers are also consumers, trade brings them immediate gains through cheaper imports; (iii) it enables most workers to become more productive as the goods they produce increase in value; (iv) trade increases technology transfers from industrial to UDCs and the transferred technology is biased in favour of skilled labour;

Increased openness to trade has been strongly associated with the reduction of poverty in most developing countries, as the historian Arnold Toynbee said 'civilisation' has been spread through 'mimesis': simple copying.

Conditions Favourable for Trade

Into the twenty-first century we 'can easily identify the conditions that are favourable for UDCs to employ foreign trade as a factor in economic growth.

Increasing spread of globalisation translates into larger movement of goods and services across the nations.

Continuing reallocation of manufacturing activities from industrial to UDCs offers ample opportunities to expand trade not only in goods, but also in services; which are becoming increasingly tradable.

Trade is interwined with another element of globalisation: the spread of international production networks.

Growth of trade is firmly butteressed by international institutions of long standing. The VWHO, built on the legacy of the GATT, aims to create a commercial environment more conducive to the multilateral exchange of goods and services.

Constraints

Most of the non-oil-producing UDCs including India, are finding themselves face to face with a number of difficulties on the foreign trade as an "engine of growth". Among these we may specifically mention the following

Slow Growth of Demand for Primary Commodities (PCs) The demand for PCs which form the principal exports of a UDC has not kept pace with the growth of world trade or with income levels in differernt countries. The world trade in PCs formed more than 50per of the total exports of the world in the year 1956. This share came down to 35 per cent in 1977 and further to 26 per sent in 2000. Four possible factors can explain the phenomenon of the fall in world trade in PCs:

The increasing tendency of the market economies to protect their agriculture by imposing tariffs and non-traiff barriers (NTBs[1]. the insistence on 'eco-labelling, or similarly the proposed German ban on the use of harmful chemicals in textile goods is the latest instance).

An inadequate increase in demand for PCs in the development market economies in the wake of industrialisation . Development of synthetic substitutes. In real terms prices of PCs are at their lowest presently over the last century and a half. [2] Growth rates are now at or near the replacement level so that little expansion can be expected from this source. Other examples of NTBs are: health and safety provisions: insistence on appreciation of currency of the supplying country (which creates automatic market constraint due to loss of competitive-ness); insistence on special information with special reference to certain items in addition to normal information supplied in the customs invoice; insistence on inspection of products by designated agencies; insistence on shipment through designated vessels and in a particular manner; insistence on the use of local materials upto a specified percentage;fixation of minimum floor prices; impos-ing unpredictable restrictions on import of inflammable products; insistence on use of certain specific materials and also ban on the use of certain specific materials. The latest addition to this list is the cumulative recovery scheme (CRS) introduced in july 1997 by EU(under the CRS, European importers of Indian Basmati.) The NTBs can be classified into two categories: technical and non-technical. Technical NTBs include such measures as a higher standard of proc-essed food industry products, food safety, non-use of certain chemical and child labour. Non-technical ones include anti-dumping duties and pre-shipment inspection. The non-technical NTBs can be contested at the WHO. See Nilanjan Hanik; "An Analysis of India's Exports during the 1990s", EPW, Vol. XXXVI, No. 44, November 9, 2001.

Competition facing important primary products:

- Primary Product Competition
- Rubber Synthetic rubber, Plastics
- Cotton Other natural and synthetic fibres
- Tin New technology pennitting thinner
- Tin plating; plastic can lining, paper
- Aluminium and plastic containers

- Jute Polypropylene and polyethylene
- Sugar High-fructose corn sweeteners
- Copper Aluminimum, Aglass fibre, plastics
- Bauxite Plastics, aluminium recycling
- Cocoa Artificial chocolate flavouring,
- vegettable oil extenders.

Slow Growth of Exports from UDCs Exports of UDCs as a grouphave been slow to-develop. As a result, the share of UDCs in the total world trade has maintained a downward trend. Thus, whereas this share was as high as 31 per cent in 1950, it came down to 14 per cent in 1960 and further to 5.9. per cent in 2000. This decline has been caused by factors like the mergence of trade blocs, restrictive commercial policies and the growth of monopolies. These trends are indicative of the fact that the UDCs have to face foreign trade as a barrier, to overcome which they may require concerted efforts.

Deteriorating Terms of Trade The declining demand for PCs in the developed markets has given rise to the problem of worsening terms of trade of the UDCs. Whereas prices of manufactured goods, specially capitial goods, have been rising in the world markets, there has been a tndency for a gradual fall in prices of primary goods. For example, according to arecent UN report, in the past UDCs could get a tractor by exporting two tonnes of sugar, now they have to export seven tonnes of sugar to get the same tractor. Any adverse foreign trade price change works as a check on economic development.

Trade policies of Developed Countries The free trade regime of the developed countries has gradually been replaced by protectionist trade regime and it is being viewed as permanent policy for times to come. Protectionist trade policies adopted. by industrial countries affect prospects for developing country exprots of manufactures. For example, even within the North American free Trade Area, High protection favours US sugar producers over Mexico exporters. The European Union is similarly discriminatory, producing unnecessary primary products and dumping them in the world market. Increased emphasis in recent years on "fair" trade by the industrialised countries, which can be viewed as a protective reaction to the serious adjustment problems these countries have them-selves faced as a consequence of increased globalisation, is a major development that tends to make it more difficult for UDCs to pull their income levels up by relying to a great extent on international trade and foreign investment. In short, UDCs face many difficulties in their foreign trade operations. The numer-ous multilateral initiatives which have left them largely unresolved. Therefore, in the given circumstances the UDCs have have to evolve a suitable trade policy-mix that may create export outlets and as well may assure supplies of essential imports.

To sum up, the composition of India's foreign trade reflects, to a great extent, the structural changes that the Indian economy has undergone over the period of last five decades. It is no longer an exporter of manufactured goods. It exports manufactured goods and imports raw materials, intermediate goods and capital goods.

Direction of India's Foreign Trade

Exports

The relative importance of the U.K and the U.S.A. as outlets for our exports has declined over the years. Whereas in 1950-51, these countries together accounted for more than 40 per cent of India's exports this share has come down presently to less than 23 per cent. The U.S.A., all the same, continues to be our principal buyer. It has, however, to contend with EU member-nations who as a group offer us a very rich market.

Alternatively, it would be seen that 60 to 65 per sent of India's im-ports consist of bulk commodities like petroleum, precious and compounds, fertilisers, etc. In other words, import management is really possible only for the balance of 35 to 40 per cent. Here again requirements of development in the form of spare parts, machinery and technology offer little scope for savings. All told the economic conditions in industrial countries significantly determine the demand for India's exports.

The export trade with the former U.S.S.R. and oter East European countries generally stimulus to exports to these countries had been provided by the mechnism of bilateral trade agreements. Of late, however, with the disintegration of the Soviet Union and the socio-economic-political changes in the former centrally-planned economies, the mechanism of bilateral agreements has broken down; presently, these countres, all told, account for a mere 3 per cent share in India's trade.

Even this is mainly due to the fact India is honouring its commitment to pepay back a total debt of the value of Rs. 30,000 crore in hard currencies over a period of 12 years beginning with 1993 to Russia.

More Recent Developments In more recent times, India's exports to Asia and Oceania markets, with whom ethnically, culturally and economically India is more closer have shown asharp jump. In fact, the current boom in exports is sustained largely by what officials see as an unexpected and healthy rise in exports to the Asia and Oceania countries, which include the ESCAP coun-tries like Australia, Iran, Japan, Korea, Malaysia, Singapore, Thailand, Hong Kong, Babgladesh and Nepal. The Shift in favour of these countries implies that Indian exporters have at least concentrated in market closer home to capitalise on the advantages from lower fright cost It is also an evidence of the outward orientation being imparted to the economy by reforms.

Imports: The direction of imports has been largely imports has been largely influnced by the development of the economy. In the initial stages of growth , a large part of the development process was financed through foreign aid which was primarily in the form of tied aid. As a result, a large part of imports originated from the aid giving countries.

In 1965-66 more than 35 percent of India's total imports come from the U.S.A Since then the share of the U.S.A has declined although it continues to be our largest supplier accounting as it does for about 8% of our total imports.

The share of the U.K in India's imports has also sharply declined although it continues to be a principlal Supplier. Among the other major coun-tries that have made inroads in our import trade are Belgium Canada , France Germany and japan. The ELT as a group accounts for about 24 percent of our imports.

Among the centrally-planned economies, the former U.S.S.R was an important purchasing centre for us. But in recent years, as already earlier noted, the importance of these countries is on the decline Russia along with other east Eureopean countries presently account for not more than 2 percent of India's total imports

A more significant development has been the emergence of oil-producing contries as a significant purchasing centre for us. This has been caused largly by sharp increase in the unit value of Petroleum and its product. The OPEC alone accounts for about 22 percent of our total imports.

Since the liberalisation in more recent years a glut of imports has began taking place from china and east Asian countries. These imports, presently, are limited to low-price consumer goods had a lion's share ranging between 51 to 62 percent of our exports and 56 to 75 percent of imports during the three decades from 1951-52 to 1979-80 In 1990-91 their share of exports aws as high as 56.7 percent while their share in imports had fallen down to 47.6 percent More recently, in 2000-01, 54.2 percent of our total exports found their destination in the EU, the USA and the UAE., Likewise, about 40.5 percent of our total imports originated from the EU, the USA and Japan. It is clear that India's for-eign trade is not diversified It means two things:

India would have to explore new sources of import and and new marker for its products in a globalising world. India need to further intensify its effort in the existing markets.

To sum up during the last five decaded significant changes have been ovserved in the volume, composition, and direction of trade Although most of these changes have been in consonance with the development needs of the econy, following problems need immediate attention

1. Problem of deficit in the balance of trade Growing trade deficits did pose problems of resources mobilation for the Indian planners rill the recent past and, therefore need be monitered continuously.
2. Our share in world trade has been showing a gradual fall. The tendency need be reversed if India is to play its rightful role in the international division of labour.

The export-led growth strategy based on translational private foreign investment, without doubt, paid rich dividends, in the newly industrialized countries (NIC). The high degree of openness and rates of growth in exports which are found to be statistically significant and positively correlated with the changes in real income coupled with consistent and sound macro-economic fiscal, monetary and exchange rates, which besides minimizing numerous regidities and distortions in the product and commodity markers (getting the prices right), distortions in the product and commodity markets (getting the prices right), discouraging rent seeking behaviour, helped them to exploit existing comparative advantages-all of them actively interplayed for the economic transformation and expansion. In other words, favourable external environment, 'getting the prices right' and getting the policies right worked in a mutually reinforcing manner for their re-markable economic performance.

However, an indepth examination of the various policies pursued by the NIC's in the past reveal that the state played an active but selected interventist role, through budget discipline, managing exchange rates, devising institutional framework marked by strong govt. discipline over the private sector and the com-plete commitment of the govt. to exports that has helped minimize the resources costs. This means that 'getting prices right' will not be enough to accelerate the process of economic growth in South including India but have to be supple-mented effectively by other well targeted protectionist policies in the different factors.

(ii) The global -economic climate which remained quite growth conducive in the 70's to some of the countries having high rates of growth of real per capita product, but seems to be less favourable and more shaky. In the near future due to global payments imbalances particularly of USA, secular revulsion of developed countries from lending resulting in shortage of liquidity and high cost of capital, slow down in the worldwide aggregate real income and output due to past disinflationary policies, which may further lead to the tightening of the availability of capital and increased protectionism, the general shifts from tariffs to non-tariff barriers viz., state participation in trade, para tariffs, specific limitations on trade flows and technical and legal regulations, and their expected unilateral in-tensification due to the fear of direct and indirect displacement in the import competing sectors having relatively, low productivity of labour. Practically, we may enter, if this trend continues, what Friedman calls into an 'era of managed trade' from an 'era of free trade'. In fact, a more or less similar situation may emerge at the international scene, if appropriate economic measures are not taken by the super economic powers, which was witnessed after the First World War when trade dependency ratios increased despite rising wave of protectionism, and the South, may become to a large extent the victin of the world deteriorating economy. Admittedly, there will be phasing out within next ten years the import quotas on textiles and cloth, in place under MFA, under the final treaty of Uru-guay Round of GATT negotiations at Marrakesh by 115 countries in April, 1994 but the fact remains that trade will play as an engine of economic growth only if all forms of 'non-tariff barriers' are reduced progressively by the advanced countries and WTO must devise Effective Dispute Settlement Procedures for cutting such abuses.

(iii) The rate of growth of an economy, in terms of Solow and Swan neo-classical growth model and Harrod and Domar growth model, given the capital-output ratio will be largely influenced by the ratio of saving to real income (S/Y) which in turn will determine the required amount of investment in order to realise planned rate of economic growth on the assumption that saving will be productively used. And obviously, a decrease in the required level of investible resources either due to external or internal factors would lead to a fall in the rate of growth. But the adverse impact of lower volume of investment, could be mitigated, by achieving a greater 'efficiency' in the use of scare investment resources, partly through a reduction in the capital-output ratio. Output and exports of manufac-tures and semi-manufactures produced efficiently would find easy and ready markets in the highly competitive markets of West where the South is simply a price taker. In fact, increasing efficiency in the use of resources in various sectors of the economy and productivity should become the centre broad economic poli-cies will act as an engine of economic growth with greater force, through the deepening of structural reforms at the internal level. "Some of the possible inter-related measures, viz, a balance between increase in productivity and increase in real wage rate, maintaining realistic and competitive exchange rates and price stability, which could be taken without much efforts, would got a long way in meeting the desired objectives.

(iv) One of the most pervasive and characteristic features of the 80's has been the remarkable renaissance of "regionalism", through the formation of trade blocks in the Europe, North America and East Asia. The GATT has sanctioned the formation of such regional groups under its article XXIV. But "Regionalism" violates the central principle of GATT of non-discrimination and cannot got certainly hand in hand with the spirit of global internationalisation. Under such a situation, the importance of increasing intra-regional trade in the developing areas currently in immense as it would, promote their collective economic growth, besides increasing and further strengthening the sense of unity and solidarity. There exists a vast scope of expanding intra-regional trade which is extremely low in the various grouping despite so many years of regional economic cooperation. The lack of complementarity and its potential erosion through the erection of tarriffs and non tarriff barriers, in the production structures, following of the self-sufficiency policies in the basic and capital goods sectors are the most important internal factors explaining the low level of intra-trade. This is quite in evidence from the low and declining values of the index RCAX./RCAM given by Balassa and Trade Intensity Index.

$$\text{RCAX} = \left(\frac{X_1^K}{X_1}\right) / \left(\frac{X_W^K}{X_W}\right)$$

$$\text{RCAM} = \left(\frac{M_1^K}{M_1}\right) / \left(\frac{M_W^K}{M_W}\right)$$

$$\text{TII} = \left(\frac{X_i j}{X_i}\right) / \left(\frac{M_j}{M_W - M}\right)$$

Where X^K is the export of product k by country iX_i is total exports of country i, X_1^K is the world exports of product k, X_W is world exports, M_i is the import of product k by country i, M_1 is total imports of country in X_1^K world imports of product k and M_W is world totahmports.

Lastly, the likely impact of emerging trends towards economic 'globlizatin during the last two decades, on 'sustainable development' in the southern areas has bccn hotly bebated Sustainable development, according to Brundtland Report (1987) is an alternative design for development which by definition is environmentally bening and eco-friendly i.e. those who reap the fruits of economic development today must not make future generations whose off by excessively degrading the earth is exhaustible resources and polutting its ecology and environment and that the resultant economic development which erodes natural of development-real income per capita which has been replaced by PQLI index, based on basic human needs due to the fact that pollution, environment and various types of acids generated due to the speeding up of the process of industrialisation and exports, have latered the chemistry of the atmosphere at a rapid pace, and given rise to various social costs which are only noted after certain time. Prof. Bhagwati (1993) is of the view of MNC's and GATT (Now WTO), NAFTA will not upset the balance a between economic progress and ecology and infact promote growth in the long run. On the other hand, Herman E Daly of World Bank and followers asserts that growth flowing from free trade will harm both environment and welfare. This seems to be true as the unrestricted operation of the MNC's may become the prime danger to environment due to (i) 'green house effect' and (ii) their ability to locate their plants in developing areas in order to escape the strict environmental standard imported by their own countries, (iii) having control to the export-oriented crops; (iv) major users of fossil fuels which releases carbon dioxide, in the atmosphere. The irresponsible use of heavy eqipments, indiscriminate cutting of forests and widespread serial spraying are sale of domestically banned, outdated and dangerous chemicals due to their having monopoly power over the natural resources, Secondly, the developing coun-tries in fact may be hard pressed to over-exploit their natural resources to meet external financial obligations which have grown exponentially, and increase exports.

And it is regretable that no existing theory of trade and WTO take into account adequately the dimension of sustainable development. The main objec-tive of liberalization and globlization at present is to achieve infinite growth in a world of finite resources, which is neither possible nor desirable. Hence, protection of environment must be a part of the guiding principles of WTO as most of the developing countries have become its members. Also it immediately calls for an active role of the state both at the national and international level to minimize the negative impact, i.e. hidden social and environmental costs of excessive trends towards globlization. In order to achieve these objectives major responsibility lies on the shoulders of advanced economics to develop new gentle and ecologically sustainable technologies, i.e., technologies which maximize the productivity of natural resources and not of labour, so that nature's infinite store-house is not exhausted. The North must set positive examples for the South that it is possible to reconciling economic prosperity with environmental problems.

The broad generalizations which emerge from the foregoing analysis, are the final success of the policies of globlization and market oriented reforms from the point of view of South's overall economic and social growth and revitalizing the future world trading order, will to a great extent, depend on the marked inprovement in the global macro-economic environment, spread of recovery from the USA to the rest of North casing the costs of adjustment process the intensity of the desire on the part of the industrialized countries to reduce NTB and over-come internal structural impediments to growth by having low rates of inflation and interest, and adjust their macro-domestic policies consistent with each other in a global framework of co-operation, and not confrontation, coupled with strong commitment and concerted efforts of South to deepen the ongoing internal reforms, increase intra-regional trade through the progressive elimination of tarrif and non-tarrit barriers, and expanding complementarity cushion, and create favourable climate for good "governance".

i. Most of the measures are basically price measures aimed improving the price competitiveness of exports. But there is a severe dearth of studies, which analyses the question of competitiveness of India's exports rigorously by segregating the price and non-price factors. Below, we discuss the little stool; of knowledge accumulated so far in the regard.

ii. Despite all the doubts expressed regarding the import-intensive content of exports, the value added, and more importantly, net foreign exchange earning of the export items, government and private efforts to carefully study these aspects have been negligible. One of the major problems seems to be the huge number of input-output coefficients that need to be-calculated in order to judge the direct indirect foreign exchange requirements of production for ex-ports or otherwise. Even then, the direct requirements should have been calcu-lated initially; only very recently the RBI and the Export Import Bank of India have undertaken some studies in this regard. However, not much serious analysis (based on such calculations) has been reported so far.

iii. One of the major problems cited in most of the government and other documents seems to be (a) lack of reforms in the non-tradable sectors which sometimes makes the domestics market relatively more profitable than export. However, these arguments are made without much theoretical insights, so that if the question arises as to what could constitutes the complementary reform of some of the non-tradable infrastructural sectors like power, communications, etc., very little sound responses can be found.

The major problem, mentioned somewhat earlier, is the rather piecemeal treatment of the non-tradable sector in the export promotion policies. It is argued that monopoly and rigid pricing in the non-tradable sectors prevents the realization of full effect of price competitiveness. This is reflected by the rather satisfactory factory movement of the measure of real exchange rate, which takes into account relative's prices of tradable and non-tradable. Hence, the question remains. What should be the proper policy towards non-tradable? A simple switching expenditure from non-tradable to tradable will not help. But if more competition in the non-tradable sector were introduced by allowing private sector participation through a judicious policy-mix regarding output and pricing, it would be more complementary to trade sector reforms. A strong infrastructure, with suitable allowances for the essential supply it needs to provide, might generate the requires flexibility in the competitive movement the real exchange rate.

Table 1 presents the result of income elasticity and price elasticity of exports for the period 1951-1994. The result should be analysed with caution beause of the possibility of serial correlation as we have used the time series data. During thus period, the income elasticity of demand for exports of food and live animals, beverages & tobacco, crude materials excluding fuels, minerals fuels etc, Animal vegetables oil, fat, chemicals retailed prod. NE's Basic manufactures, machines transport, misc manufactured goods and total exports took the expected positive sign and it is significant. This confirms that globlisation of the Indian Economy with the rest of the world would be useful as there is sufficient foreign demand for Indian exports. Since, integration of the economy would make the economy cost efficient the demand for exports will increase more and thus India would be able to earn adequate foreign exchange in order to finance its import bill. As for as the price elasticity of demand for exports is concerned the coefficient took the unexpected positive sign in all cases. This shows that the 5 are distortions in the various sectors of the economy which can be removed through liberalization and globlisation.

Price elasticity and income elasticity of demand for exports of India according to SITC 1951-1994.

Table-1

Dependent variable	*CONST.*	*LNRGDP*	*ADJ R^2*	*F-VALUE*
Food Animal	0.86	0.228	0.38	9.47
Beverage & Tobaco	2.99	0.333	0.22	
Crude Material Excluding fuels	0.23	0.773	0.628	23.85
Mineral Fuels	0.58	-0.126	0.007	7.09
Animal Veg. Oil	0.16	-0.139	0.29	6.66
Chemical Retailed Prod. NE's	1.98	0.392	0.43	11.35
Basic Manufacture	2.99	0.152	0.39	9.87
Machines	4.36	1.016	0.79	54.98
Transport Goods	1.99	0.546	0.55	17.94
Total Exports	2.64	0.208		

Table-2

Dependent variable	*CONST.*	*LNRGDP*	*ADJ R^2*	*F-VALUE*
Food and live Animal	9.899	-0.677	0.02	1.345
Beverage and Tobacco	21.229	-2.196	0.49	14.436
Crude materials Excluding Fuel	-6.372	0.692	0.28	6.280

Mineral Fuels	-18.511	1.895	0.55	18.072
Animal Veg. oil, fat	-58.318	5.062	0.80	54.988
Chemicals Related Prod.	-20.956	1.997	0.78	49.747
Basic Manufacture	-12.076	1.251	0.40	10.203
Machines, Transport	-0.164	0.255	0.002	0.963
Misc. Manufactured Goods	-13.837	1.236	0.241	5.304
Total Imports	-6.181	0.915	0.64	25.326

Estimation of income and price elasticities of imports of India : 1951-1994.

Table 2 presents the income and price elasticities of imports of India for the period 1951-1994. The income elasticity of demand for imports took the expected positive sign in all the cases. This implies that with increase international income, imports will go up as revealed by the international trade theory. There fore the best policy is to liberalise the imports as they also act as a critical inpu for most of our exports. The price-elasticity of demand for imports took the ex pected negative sign in all the cases. But it is not significant statiscally.

The careful analysis of these tables reveal that Indian economy does have the necessary attributes for the success of market mechanism and recent changes in the trade policy in an attempt to liberate and intergate it with the rest of the world, would prove fruitful and productive. Some more data after these policy changes, is required.

This establishes that foreign trade plays an important role in economic development in Inida. The income elasticity of demand for exports/imports of India is greater than one and sufficiently high. This emphasized the nee for globlisation of the Indian economy.

The price elasticity of demand for exports/imports is also importan but not always. But in some cases, it is statistically significant. This implies tha Market-Mechanism can be helpful and made operative in India. For this mor liberalised trade policy is needed. Hence, we feel strongly that recent steps taken by the government towards globlisation and libralisation would yield productiv results.

BIBLIOGRAPHY

1. P.T. Ellsworth and J. Clark Leith, The International Economy, Fifth Edition, 1975, pp. 89-92 and pp. 187-191, Chapter 9 and 11.
2. H. Robert Heller, International Trade, Second Edition, 1973, Chapter 8
3. Charles P. Kindlergerger, International Economics, Fifth Edition, 1973, Chapter 5, pp. 75-75
4. Gerald P. Kindlerberger, International Economics, Fifth Edition, 1973, Chapter 5, pp. 33-76
5. Jaroslav Vanek, Studies in the Theory of International Trade, 1962, Chapter 16
6. Jackob Vinner, Studies in the Theory of International Trade, 1937, Chapters VIII and IX
7. Charles P. Kindlergerger, International Economics, Fifth Edition, 1973, p.156
8. F.F. Hechscher, "Utrikeshandelns verkan pa inkomstfordelnigen, Ekonomisk Tidskrift, 1919 (reprint in English translation in TRIT)
9. B. Ohlin, Interregional and International Trade, Cambridge, Mass, Havard University Press, 1933, especially ch 4 and 7.
10. R.W. Jones, "Factor Proportions and the Hechscher-Ohlin Teorem, Res, January, 1956.

11. P. A. Samuelson, "Internatioal Trade and the Equalization of Factor Prices", EJ, June, 1948.

12. P.A. Samuelson, "International Factor-Price Equalization One Again", EJ, June 1949 (reprinted in RIE)

13. H.G.Johso, "Factor Endowments, International Trade and Factor of Prices. MS. September; 1957 (Reprint in RIE)

14. K. Lancaster, "The Hechscher-Ohlin Trade Model: A Geometric Treatment, Ec, February 1957.

15. J.L. Mosak, General Equilibrium Theory in International, Bloomington, Indiana, Principia Press, 1972

16. T. Negeshi, General Equillibrium Theory and International Trade, Amsterdam, North Holland, 1972.

17. R. W. Jones, "Factor Proportions and the Hechscher-Ohlin Teorem, Res January, 1956.

18. I.F. Pearce, International Trade, London, Macmiillan, 1970, Book 11, Chapter 16.

19. M.C.Kemp, The Pure theory of International Trade and Investment, Engles wood Cliffs, N.J., Prentice Hall, 1969.

20. J. Bhagwati, "The pure Theories in International Trade EJ, Vol, 74 March 1964.

21. Robert M. Stem, "Testing Trade Theories in International Trade and Finance. Frontiers for Research, Cambridege University, Press, 1975.

22. R.E. Baldwin and J. B. Richardson eds, International Trade and Finnce, Readings, Boston, Little Brown, 1973.

23. Robert E. Baldwin, "Determinants of the Commodity Structed AFR March 1971.

24. K.E.Hanson, "A General Theory of the System of Multilateral Trade, "AEF, Vol. 42, March 1952, p. 52

25. Vanek, "The Natural Resources Content of Foreign Trade, 1870-1955 and the Relative Abundance of Natural Resources in the United States, RE K& S, Vol. 41, May 1959, pp. 166.

26. R. E. Caves, "Export-led Growth and the New Economic History." in J Bhagwati et al, Trade Balance of Payments and Growth, Amsterdam, 1971.

27. R. Frindlay, Vent for Surplus, "Models of Trade and Growth", in R.E. Baldwin et al., 1965

28. S.A. Resnik, "The Decline of Rural Industry under Export Expansion : a Comparision among Burma, Philippines and Thailand, 1879-1938. Journal of Economic History, March 1970

29. M.A. Adelman, The world Petrolem Market, Baltimore, 1973.

30. D. L. McLachaln and D. Swann, Competition Policy in the European Compunity, London.

31. J. A. Suhumpeter, "Zur Soziologie der Imperialismen", Archiv fur Sociolwisenchaft (1919), Volume 46, p. 301,

32. Gottfried Von Haberler, op, cit., p. 314

33. P.T. Ellsworth and J.C. Leith, International Economy, Fifth Edition, 1975, p. 250.

34. Brahamananda, P.R. : The Lakdawala Merorial Lecture, Economic of India's International Integration (Indian Economic Conference at Indore 1993)

35. Panchmukhi V.R. Recent Developments in Trade theory and Practice, Presidential Address, Platinum Ju bileeAnnual Conference of the Indian Eco nomic Association, Bombay 94.

36. Panchmukhi V.R. The Emerging internation Trading Order, RIS Digest, Sept. 93.

37. Manmohan Singh : Iadia's Exports Trends and Prospect of Self Sustained Growth, Clarendon, 1964.

38. Balassa (1965) : "Tariff Protection in Industrial Countries: An Evaluation : Journal of Political Economy, I, XXIII. 579-94

39. Balassa (1968) : "Tariff Protection in Industrial Nations and its Effects on the Exports of Processed Goods from Developing Countries", Canadian Journal of Economics, 1. 583-594.

40. E. Baldwin (1952) : "The New Welfare Economics and Gains in Inter-national Trade", Quartely Journal of Economics., I. XVI. 91-101

41. Barker (1977) : "International Trade and Economic Growth : An Alternative to the Neo-Classical Approach", Cambride Journal of Economics, l, 153-72

42. J. Bhagwati (1969) : "On the Equivalence of Tariffs and Quotas", in Trade Tariff and Growth, (London, Weidenfeld and-licholson.)

43. J. Bhagwati (1971) : "The Pure Theory of International Trade : A Survey', in Trade, Tariffs and Growth", (London, Weidenfeld and Nicholson.)

44. R. Caves (1981) : "Intra-Industry Trade and Market Structure in the Industrial Countries", Oxford Economic Papers, XXXIII, 203-23.

45. R. Caves & H.G. : Readings in International Economics (London, Jonhson (eds.) (1968) Allen and Unwin.)

46. J. M. Finger (1974) : "GATT Tariff Concessions and the Exports of Developing Countries Countries", US Concessions at the Kennedy Round", Economic Journal, I,XXXIV, 566-75

47. C. Frank (1977) : Foreign Trade and Domestic Aid (Washington, Brookings Institution).

48. M. Friedman (1977) : "Noble Lecture : Inflation and Unemployment", Journal of Political Economy, I.XXXV, 451-72.

49. H.G. Grubel & H.G. : Effective Tariff Protection (Geneva, Graduate Johnson (eds) (1968) Institute of International Studies.

50. G. Heberler (1950) : "Some Problems in the Pure Theory of Interna-tional Trade:, Economic Journal, LX, 223-40

51. E. Heckscher (1919)_ "The Effects of Foreign Trade on the Distribution of Income", Economic Tidskrift, reprinted in H. Ellis and L.A. Metzler (eds) (1948) Readings in the Theory of International Trade (Homewood, Illinois, Irwin)

52. G. Hufbauer and "Specialisation by Industrial Countries: Extent and J. Chilas (1974) Consequences", in H. Gierschfed. The Interna-tional Division of Labour, Problems and Perspectives (Tubingen, J.C.B. Mohr).

53. H.G. Johnson (1950-1): "Optimum Welfare and Maximum Revenue Tarrits" , Review of Economic Studies, XIX, 28-35

54. L.B. Krause (1959) : U.S. Imports and the "Tariff, Amerian Economic Review, XLIX, 542-51

55. P. Krugman (1979) : "Increasing Returns, Monopolistic Completion and International Trade", Journal of Interna-tional Economics, IX, 469-79

56. W. Leontief (1953) : "Domestic Production and Foreign Trade : the Amerian Capital Position Re-examined", Economia Internationale, VII, 3-32

57. S.B. Linder (1961) : An Essay on Trade and Transformation (New York, John Wiley).

58. R.G. Lipsey and "The General Theory of Second Best",Review of Lancaster (1956-57) Economic Studies, XXIV, 11032.

59. M. V. Posner (1961) : "Technical Change and International Trade", Oxford Economic Papers, XIII, 323-41

60. D. Ricardo (1817) : The principles of Political Economy and Taxation (London, Dent edition 1973)

61. P.A. Samuelson (1939): "The Gains from International Trade", Canadian Journal of Economics and Political Science, V, 195-205

62. P.A Samuelson (1948): "The Gains from Internation Trade", Economics Journal LVIII, 163-84

63. R.M. Stern (1975) : "Testing Trade Theories", in P.B. Kenen (ed.). International Trade and Finance (Cambridge, Cambridege University Press)